Driving Social Change

Driving Social Change

How to Solve the World's Toughest Problems

Paul C. Light

Foreword by Catherine B. Reynolds

John Wiley & Sons, Inc.

Published by John Wiley & Sons, Inc., Hoboken, New Jersey.
Published simultaneously in Canada.

For general information on our other products and services or for technical support, please contact our Customer Care Department within the United States at (800) 762-2974, outside the United States at (317) 572-3993 or fax (317) 572-4002.

Wiley also publishes its books in a variety of electronic formats. Some content that appears in print may not be available in electronic books. For more information about Wiley products, visit our web site at www.wiley.com.

Library of Congress Cataloging-in-Publication Data:

Light, Paul Charles.
Driving social change : how to solve the world's toughest problems / Paul C. Light.
p. cm.
Includes bibliographical references and index.
ISBN 978-0-470-92241-5 (cloth); ISBN 978-0-470-94013-6 (ebk);
ISBN 978-0-470-94012-9 (ebk); ISBN 978-0-470-94014-3 (ebk)
1. Social change. 2. Social problems. 3. Infrastructure (Economics) I. Title.
HM831.L54 2010
303.48'4—dc22

2010032315

Printed in the United States of America

10 9 8 7 6 5 4 3 2 1

To Ernie, who took me across the finish line

Contents

Foreword

Simply defined, social entrepreneurship creates new combinations of ideas that spur solutions to great problems. It is an essential path to doing well and doing good at the same time.

It is also a time-honored form of leadership. Social entrepreneurs do not spend their time telling others what to do. They pick up the reins. They keep the plates spinning toward achieving an impact. They have the drive to tackle social issues through all means possible. Social entrepreneurs are not cynics. They believe they can change the world.

Social entrepreneurs are not wed to any particular method, however. They do whatever is necessary to make a difference for the public good and they operate across society. Some work in nonprofit agencies, others in government, and still others in private firms.

Wherever they work, social entrepreneurs must have the business savvy, financial skills, and innovative passion to disrupt the status quo of our social problems and thereby create large-scale change. There is always something to disrupt, but not always the strategy needed for the long drive for success.

At the heart of every breakthrough is an outside-the-box visionary who had a passion for making a difference. It is true in science, the arts, education, and business—and it is true in solving social problems.

Think of the business entrepreneurs who changed the United States. Henry Ford did it with the Model T, a car for the masses. George Eastman did it with photography. A. P. Giannini did it with his branch banking idea for all citizens, rich or poor, and modern banking was the result. And a young professor of molecular biology named Herbert Boyer endured academic scorn by going into business to produce synthetic hormones and launch an ongoing biotech revolution.

Why can't the same out-of-the-box approach be used for social problems?

What if we found people with the same drive and courage as Herb Boyer to address widespread social ills?

Paul C. Light has important answers to these questions. Like me, he believes in the power of the individual to make a difference. Like me, he believes in the power of innovation to make a difference. And, like me, he believes that social change is not only possible, but essential for addressing the great problems that surround us.

Let me highlight three change agents, true social entrepreneurs who embody this potent combination.

A social entrepreneur from Bangladesh, Muhammad Yunus, won the Nobel Peace Prize for creating and expanding his trailblazing use of small loans, or microcredit, to bring about social change. Loans as low as $9 have helped beggars start small businesses and poor women buy basket-weaving materials.

As the Nobel Committee said in its citation, "Lasting peace cannot be achieved unless large population groups find ways in which to break out of poverty. Microcredit is one such means."

The founder of the American Association of Retired Persons (now AARP), Ethel Percy Andrus, was an equally important but less visible social entrepreneur. She saw the need to bring older persons out of their isolation and back into the mainstream of American life and created AARP to achieve her goal. Today, AARP has 40 million members who receive a variety of benefits that have improved the quality of their lives and the economic vitality of the United States. Andrus gave voice to the needs and opportunities of millions of older Americans.

My friend Wendy Kopp, for her senior thesis as an undergraduate at Princeton University, envisioned a movement that would fill the empty classrooms in the nation's most needy schools. She turned her thesis into the organization Teach for America, which now places more than 7,000 corps members in classrooms across the nation. Over the past 20 years, Teach for America alumni have reached approximately three million students. In doing so, she touched a nerve with college students who want to make a difference in American education.

Why did the world get so excited when Warren Buffett said he was going to give $31 billion of his stock to the Bill & Melinda Gates Foundation? I have thought about that a good deal. The excitement was not just about the money—after all, government has much more money that either Buffett or Gates.

Rather, it was about new ways to meet old social problems. It was also about supporting new ideas for tackling large problems. And it was about creating and expanding big ideas.

Let me tell you about the nature of social entrepreneurs by relating a story about the behavior of birds.

There was an article a number of years ago in the *Harvard Business Review* that had to do with successful companies. One interesting analogy the author used regarded the behavior of two species of birds, brown titmice and red robins, in Great Britain.

In the late 1800s, milkmen left open bottles of milk on people's doorsteps. The rich cream would rise to the top, and the titmice and robins would consume the cream.

In the 1930s, after the birds had been enjoying the cream for about 50 years, the British began to put aluminum seals on the bottles. By the early 1950s, the entire population of an estimated one million titmice had learned to pierce the seals. The robins never acquired that skill.

Now why is that? The answer is that robins are territorial. There is a great deal of communication among them but it is usually of the "keep out of my territory" variety. The titmice, in contrast, like to flock. And birds that flock learn faster.

Social entrepreneurs are like titmice. Yes, entrepreneurs are independent birds, but they do flock—they flock toward new ideas and others of their kind who have new ideas.

They share. They compare. They experiment. They try this. They try that. They cock their heads and look at the seal until they figure out how to break it and get the cream.

Light's new book shows us how social entrepreneurs and other change agents can use the same kind of creative collaboration to achieve social change. Like social entrepreneurs, he is not wed to any one path to having an impact.

He believes that change can come from the kind of visible heroes my foundation supports through the Academy of Achievement, from pathbreaking institutions such as Teach for America, from teams of talented individuals who work together toward sustaining and protecting social breakthroughs, and from collections of change agents who form networks for sharing ideas and promoting impact. And perhaps most important, he believes that power is an essential resource in creating change.

His book offers a number of important insights for creating future breakthroughs toward economic, social, and political progress. He rightly argues that our fundamental purpose must be to change the world. Social entrepreneurship has never been about personal glory, though glory sometimes follows. It is about the tough work of change.

Light also rightly argues that there are many partners in successful change. There is almost always a visible figure at the front of the march, but there must be others walking side by side. Change rarely occurs through the simple power of a good idea—it requires hard work by many people who share the same goal. The path to change must follow the ultimate goal, not vice versa.

Finally, Light argues that we must learn more about how to make the best use of our change agents. They face many obstacles on the path to success. As I have learned firsthand, the status quo often uses every means possible, including the aggressive use of power, to resist change. That is how it remains the status quo.

Light's book offers other insights about how change occurs, including the need for constant vigilance regarding past achievements such as women's rights, environmental protection, and reducing disease. We must simultaneously push forward with new solutions to old problems, while protecting past breakthroughs that continue to produce progress. As Light argues, this is not an either-or world. We must alter the future even as we celebrate the past.

I commend Light's book to anyone dedicated to social change. His questions deserve answers, his insights demand attention, and his faith in the possible will resonate with the future leaders who are already taking the reins of power needed for solving the world's toughest problems.

Catherine B. Reynolds
Chairman of the Board
Catherine B. Reynolds Foundation
July 31, 2010

Acknowledgments

This book is the inaugural contribution of my New York University Center for Global Public Service and Social Change. The center is jointly sponsored by New York University and the government of the United Arab Emirates. Its mission is to promote public service and social change across the globe, and it will draw upon research, case studies, and networks to advance efforts to address the world's toughest problems, which are often called *urgent threats*.

This book could not have been written without support for the new center. This support was awarded through a competitive process at New York University, and benefited greatly from input from senior New York University officers, most notably Provost David McLaughlin and Deputy Provost Ron Robin. This work also benefited from the support of the dean of the Robert F. Wagner School of Public Service, Ellen Schall, and associate deans Rogan Kersh and Tyra Liebmann, and the talented staff that provided the administrative support for this work. I also received significant encouragement from the director of the Catherine B. Reynolds Program in Social Entrepreneurship and its director,

Gabriel Brodbar, and interactions with colleagues at Duke University and Oxford University's 2010 Research Forum on Social Entrepreneurship.

I am also grateful to the many colleagues who have participated in conversations about social change, including Paul Davis, Susan Davis, J. Gregory Dees, James Dewar, Bill Drayton, Cynthia Gibson, Peter Goldberg, Rich Harwood, Robert Lempert, Joe Magee, Ruth McCambridge, Ellen McGrath, Jonathan Morduch, Sonia Ospina, Ed Skloot, Dan Smith, and Dennis Smith, and to the many students who have shaped my thinking through their tough questions. I am particularly thankful for ongoing encouragement from my friend and mentor Joel Fleishman.

I owe a special debt of gratitude to my alma matter, Macalester College, which invited me to present an earlier version of this book in February 2010. My former professors at "Mac" were instrumental in teaching me how to think about social change, in no small measure because Mac created a learning culture for its students.

Ultimately, this book could not have been written without frequent questions from my talented research team, which is ably led by my deputy, Clara Janis, and my research assistants, Nick Farrell and Steven Friday. I also deeply appreciate the team at John Wiley & Sons, who acted with speed and great attention to quality. As always, however, this book is mine and mine alone. I am responsible for errors, assertions, and facts herein.

Introduction

The world faces an onslaught of urgent threats. Poverty continues to corrode hope and opportunity, disease threatens lives and well-being, intolerance marginalizes hundreds of millions and fuels genocide, political instability and corruption produce failed states and genocide, global warming continues its onward march toward environmental devastation, the global recession maintains a tight grip on inequality, and the world remains vulnerable to a host of known and yet-to-be-known catastrophes.

These threats are urgent if only because the world has little time to act before reaching tipping points that will create decades, if not centuries, of havoc. They threaten the very fabric of the world's social, economic, and political systems, and almost certainly guarantee a declining quality of life for every citizen. They must be tackled soon.

The cover of this book makes this point perfectly. The leaves of social breakthroughs are part of the trees of new and still-vibrant breakthroughs alike, and the trees are part of the forest of change. Every leaf is nurtured by the forest as a whole, and is linked in some way to the broader effort to move from the darkness of winter through the many colors leading to a vibrant spring. The challenge is to reach the green and hold it, in part by supporting the forest as a whole.

This book is based on the notion that intractable problems can be solved if agents of change have the purpose and perseverance to confront the status quo. The path to a more just, tolerant, and equitable world is never easy, but its twists and turns can be marked and informed.

Drawing upon my own research and new insights from recent studies, the book asks three sets of questions.

- First, are we relying too heavily on lone wolves to produce social entrepreneurship and change? How do we end the definitional debate about what does and does not constitute change? And what is the entrepreneur's role in protecting past breakthroughs? Simply asked, are we overselling social entrepreneurship as the primary, or even only, driver of social breakthroughs?
- Second, what are other drivers that can be used for social change? How do they work? What is their role in pushing through the key stages of impact? And where do they fit in the breakthrough cycle? Simply asked, have we neglected other actors in both challenging the prevailing wisdom, addressing urgent threats, and honoring the promises we make?
- Third, how do breakthroughs actually occur? What are the key steps in creating momentum toward disruption, breakthrough, and durable social change? What are the most promising targets for further research and investment? And what are the essential characteristics of robust movement through the breakthrough cycle? Simply asked, how can collaboration advance success?

Although each chapter stands separately, they all relate to the breakthrough cycle discussed in Chapter 3. Social entrepreneurship is a critically important part of the agitation needed for change, as are social safekeeping, exploring, and advocating. So is the infrastructure of change that supports social breakthrough. Viewed as a whole, this book focuses on the overall pieces that must come together to solve the world's toughest problems.

Along the way, the book focuses on the need to protect past social breakthroughs from complacency and counterattack. Unlike business breakthroughs that sweep away entire industries with a single product, social breakthroughs rarely destroy the industries of deprivation that profit from human suffering. These industries not only survive most breakthroughs; they sometimes return to power in the very next election or war.

Defining Breakthrough

Social breakthrough is a nearly perfect term for describing the ultimate output of social action. When successful, social breakthrough pushes a fundamental change in the prevailing wisdom about who gets what, when, where, and how from a society. Social breakthrough occurs when the demand for an end to deprivation, marginalization, and inequality finally overwhelms the resistance. Some breakthroughs involve the faithful execution of new laws and treaties, others create measurable changes in public behavior, and still others actually dismantle a whole industry of deprivation by restoring human rights and liberties.

However, social breakthrough is not a synonym for social entrepreneurship or innovation. Rather, it is the destination of all social action, and involves a cycle of engagement that can act as a map for deploying resources and energy. Although a breakthrough can come from the new combinations of ideas that underpin innovation (social entrepreneurship), it can also come from the aggressive defense, delivery, and expansion of past breakthroughs (social safekeeping), careful research on trends and solutions (social exploring), and the unrelenting demand for change embedded in social networks (social advocacy). The choice of one driver over another depends entirely on the problem to be solved, not the popularity of a particular approach. The urgent threat comes first, while the choice of a particular driver for achieving impact comes second. Form follows function, path follows purpose, and driver follows destination, not vice versa.

As such, we must search for change through all means possible, whether beneath the lamppost that illuminates individual heroes or just beyond the light among those who aggregate the pressure for change. If our purpose is to change the world, we must concentrate on every driver possible, not just the ones we can see.

A Sheldonian Moment

Ironically perhaps, I came to this conclusion after attending the three-day 2009 Skoll World Forum on Social Entrepreneurship, which took place in Oxford, England. It was a remarkable event—intense, inspiring, and engaging. All the people I admire were there—Bill Drayton, Pamela Hartigan, Darell Hammond, Victoria Hale, Sally Osberg, Larry Brilliant, and even Jeff Skoll himself. I attended the forum ready to embrace social entrepreneurship as the key driver of social breakthrough and did everything I could to make the conversion. But the event convinced me otherwise.

On the one hand, the forum offered plenty of inspiration through stories and films about the heroes who work so hard to achieve social breakthroughs. The forum also featured grants to a host of social entrepreneurs, such as Bart Weetjans of Apopo, Nader Khateeb and Gidon Bromberg from EcoPeace, Martin von Hildebrand from Foudación Gaia Amazonas, Nina Smith from GoodWeave (formerly known as Rugmart International), and Jordan Kassalow from VisionSpring (formerly known as Scojo).

On the other hand, the forum was unsettling. Perhaps it was just the contrarian in me. Or perhaps it was Jeff Skoll's speech about the state of the world. The more Skoll talked about the urgent threats facing the world, the more I wanted to be anywhere but in the historic Sheldonian Theatre where he spoke. So much money and celebration for so many wonderful start-ups—but so many frightening problems and so much deep uncertainty about the future.

The two themes are now coming together, in part because Skoll and other funders are focusing more closely on collaboration. As the Skoll Foundation argued in announcing its 2010 world forum, heroes will always be an essential source of new combinations of ideas, but *catalytic collaboration* is the key to eventual impact:

> More and more social entrepreneurship is not only about the power of the brilliant individual; increasingly it's about the power of partnerships, the coalitions that take the solutions you envision and bring the impact of those solutions to scale, not necessarily one organization to scale, the impact of the solution to scale. This is the direction we are headed, toward a dynamic open-source model of social breakthrough.

Catalytic collaboration is also an essential tool for achieving scale, which means harnessing enough momentum and power to bring about change. Scale is not about becoming a super-sized organization, but about achieving impact. Defined as such, scaling involves a very different set of skills beyond fund-raising and organizational development. It involves "swarming a target," playing political hardball, setting the agenda, exploiting leverage points, creating coalition where credit is shared rather than hoarded, and fighting back when the old equilibrium begins its inevitable counterattack. Social entrepreneurs surely know how to take punches—this is part of challenging the prevailing wisdom. They need to know how to deliver punches, too.

By definition, an open-source model is both porous and flexible. It cannot be an invitation-only mechanism restricted just to social entrepreneurs. It must involve every source of energy—the entrepreneurs who create new combinations of ideas; the social explorers who monitor the trends and opportunities; the social advocates who twist arms and count votes; and the social safekeepers who protect, repair, reinvent, and implement great breakthroughs.

Structure of the Book

This book is best read as my latest report from the conversation about social change. Although the book focuses first on the role of social entrepreneurship as a powerful source of new ideas, it also examines other, equally powerful drivers of social change that participate in the social breakthrough cycle.

According to many advocates of change, social entrepreneurship is the primary tool for challenging the prevailing wisdom about the human condition. But there are also old ideas that merit protection, innovation, and expansion. There has already been great progress on pulling individuals out of poverty, treating life-threatening diseases, and addressing barriers to equal rights. Social entrepreneurship offers hope for new ways of achieving great social goals, but so do social safekeeping, exploring, and advocacy.

Chapter 1: Still Searching for Social Entrepreneurship

This first chapter of this book addresses the rapidly changing definition of social entrepreneurship. Having studied the term for nearly eight years now, I remain committed to the concept. New combinations of ideas matter. However, the more I study the term, and its links to other terms such as *social innovation*, which I wrote about in the early 1990s, the more I resist the exclusive approach often used in the field.

My definition of the new social entrepreneurship (circa 2011) is as simple as possible: Social entrepreneurship is an essential but not exclusive driver of innovative social breakthrough. Again, it is an important driver, to be sure, and one with great potential. At the same time, it is not always the best driver for solving a given problem. Again, driver follows destination.

The chapter also explores the assumptions that underpin our understanding of social entrepreneurship—for example, the notion that social entrepreneurs usually work alone, are different from other high achievers, work in similar ways, and produce their greatest impact in new, small, and often isolated organizations. While several of these assumptions are true—social entrepreneurs do have special skills for change, for example—several are still in play.

As the chapter argues, for example, social entrepreneurship may actually come in several flavors, including "Type A" social entrepreneurship driven by the heroic, 24/7 lone wolf working within a start-up organization, and the less prominent "Type B" social entrepreneurship ignited by collaborative creativity across teams working within an existing setting. The choice of one type over another should depend entirely on the overall strategy for achieving social breakthrough—again, driver follows destination.

Chapter 2: Agitating the Prevailing Wisdom

The second chapter of this book argues that social entrepreneurship exists in a world of many options for change, including three other powerful, often neglected drivers of social breakthrough: social safekeeping, social exploring, and social advocacy. When combined with social entrepreneurship, the three increase the odds that new and old ideas alike will actually penetrate the prevailing equilibrium and survive.

Each of these four drivers has its own role in social change:

1. If the breakthrough requires a new combination of ideas for change, then social entrepreneurship is likely to be the preferred driver.
2. If the breakthrough demands the protection, repair, maintenance, fine-tuning, expansion, and further innovation of past breakthroughs, then social safekeeping is likely to be at the forefront.
3. If the breakthrough stands on an effort to anticipate key threats, monitor trends, and evaluate what does and does not work, then social exploring is likely to be the means to the end.

4. If the breakthrough achieves ultimate policy impact through lobbying, pressure, partisanship, and long-lasting social movement, then social advocacy must be engaged.

This second chapter begins with a definition of social safekeeping as a contributor to social change. The term is particularly appealing as an alternative to *social service provision*, which is often used to describe the day-to-day delivery of public goods and services. Contrasted with the heroic social entrepreneur, social service providers become little more than metaphorical cafeteria workers of a kind who serve the same tired food on metal trays each morning. Safekeeping challenges this traditional, sometimes unintended but still dismissive image through a job description that includes the execution, defense, repair, innovation, and expansion of breakthroughs. On the notion that the best offense is a good defense, social safekeepers must be proactive in defending the past but never protect it from needed change.

The chapter then introduces the concept of social exploring, which encompasses a range of tools for understanding past successes, anticipating alternative futures, and testing vulnerable assumptions. These exploratory tools are central for creating, hedging, and shaping strategies for achieving desired futures. They are also essential for avoiding surprise. As a professor of mine once told me, "It's what you don't even know that you don't know that can hurt you." Social exploring provides the tools for knowing.

The chapter continues with a short discussion of social advocacy as a tool for creating breakthroughs, and turns to the concept of *blended agitation* as a way to bring together the unique strengths of all four drivers of social change.

The chapter ends with a discussion of the need to protect the great breakthroughs that social entrepreneurs have already created. Past breakthroughs do not sustain themselves, especially in an era of retrenchment and complacency. We too often assume that past breakthroughs will take care of themselves, but unlike business entrepreneurship, which often renders existing products obsolete for good, social change is painfully easy to reverse.

Chapter 3: The Breakthrough Cycle

The third chapter of this book describes the social breakthrough cycle, which provides a new approach for framing the debate about urgent threats. The cycle is built rather like the traditional links in a logic chain, albeit with a continuous plan-do-check-act rotation. However, unlike a traditional logic chain composed of inputs, activities, outputs, and outcomes, the social breakthrough cycle involves nine stages:

1. Committing to social change through personal purpose and perseverance against potential resistance.
2. Mapping the assets and obstacles surrounding success, while developing strategies for exploiting the former and surmounting the latter.
3. Sorting the potential components of a breakthrough proposal.
4. Designing a breakthrough proposal and finding an organizational home for pursuing change.
5. Agitating the prevailing wisdom through social entrepreneurship, safekeeping, exploring, and/or advocacy.
6. Aggregating pressure for change through the creation of robust breakthrough networks.
7. Disrupting the prevailing wisdom by exploiting opportunities for impact and planning for effects.

8. Securing the breakthrough through formal and informal enactment of the breakthrough idea, whether in the form of significant policy change or new norms and expectations for a just world.
9. Protecting the breakthrough from counterattack.

This breakthrough cycle is anything but linear—there are starts and stops along the way, fine-tuning, reassessments of earlier decisions, and new calibrations of strategy in response to changing opportunities and conditions.

The chapter continues with discussions of five particularly important leverage points for creating a new prevailing wisdom: committing, mapping, designing, aggregating, and disrupting. It is nearly impossible, for example, to activate the social breakthrough cycle without a basic commitment to making a difference, nor create momentum forward without assets such as civic demand for change, basic freedom to act, government responsiveness, and faithful execution of the laws.

The chapter ends with a discussion of how to build a robust breakthrough cycle. Some cycles lack the basic capacity to succeed—they lack the alertness to anticipate emerging trends, the agility to exploit opportunities and react to counterattacks, the adaptability to alter strategy midstream, and the alignment to pull disparate interests into a sum greater than the parts.

Chapter 4: Prepare to Expect Wonders

The final chapter provides a short list of findings and recommendations for steering the conversation about social breakthrough. If I have a single recommendation at the top of this book, it is to stop drawing sharp lines between the four drivers of lasting change (social entrepreneurship, safekeeping, exploring, and advocacy), and start building the social networks that play such a key role in the breakthrough cycle. It is no longer enough to imagine and launch bold ideas for solving tough problems. We must also turn possibilities into deep disruptions and breakthroughs.

The conclusion also examines the current condition of the social breakthrough infrastructure, which is essential to both creating and sustaining breakthroughs. Social change does not occur in a vacuum—it is incubated, expanded, and accelerated by a larger infrastructure. Unfortunately, the infrastructure of change is under siege. It is often the first cut and the last investment during periods of intense economic stress.

Lessons Learned

This book draws upon my own journey through the thicket of social change over the past 30 years. If this journey has taught me one thing, it is that social change does not occur in any one sector with any single driver at any specific moment. Change involves an ongoing effort both within and across the sector boundaries, the four drivers, and a long-haul philosophy.

This is only one of the many lessons I learned from my sawtooth journey. Consider six others.

First, social breakthrough cannot occur without a commitment to civic leadership in all its forms, be it full-time, part-time, or occasional, by lone wolves, teams, or networks. Some citizens create social breakthrough by what we are now calling micro-volunteering, which involves very small acts of conscience. Others create impact through very traditional engagement, which involves traditional political activities such as voting, paying attention to the news, writing letters to the editor and members of Congress, and working for campaigns. And still others engage in what we sometimes call strong democracy, thick engagement, or engaged citizenship, all of which are terms that capture forms of advocacy such as protesting, petitioning, litigating, testifying (in many ways), declaring, and so forth. But whatever the form of engagement, the commitment to make a difference, big or small, is at the core of the breakthroughs that redefine the prevailing wisdom.

Second, as the Skoll Foundation and so many other experts argue, social breakthrough almost always occurs through collaboration, partnerships, networks, and even social movements. As I argue in Chapter 1, the field of social entrepreneurship spends too much time focusing on individual heroes, and not enough on the networks forged between and among citizens and communities through grassroots tactics. These partnerships are essential for massing enough power to start the great engines of impact such as movements, campaigns, and even lobbying. We cannot avoid it—power and politics are central to addressing the urgent threats now barreling down on us.

Third, social change must be firmly anchored in what constitutional founder Alexander Hamilton called "extensive and arduous enterprises for the public benefit." It is the enterprise, not the driver, that matters most for ultimate success in creating a new prevailing wisdom. Social entrepreneurs, safekeepers, explorers, and advocates must be ready to submerge themselves in the overall campaign for change. Much as everyone might want a bit of recognition and thanks along the way, they cannot let this desire, and the funding that often goes with it, become an end in itself.

Fourth, breakthrough does not always require a new organization led by a celebrated hero. Even ancient organizations can create change, and they need not do so through 24/7 engagement. Creating innovative ideas within existing organizations, particularly giant ones, is not easy. Inventing from within is difficult, frustrating, and often unsuccessful. But its value is obvious: Large, old organizations have resources, whether for demonstration projects, education and lobbying, dissemination and replication, or defense against counterattacks.

Fifth, higher education must play a more aggressive and unified role in educating the next generation of change agents. Higher education is moving toward the long-needed transformation from a dry, bureaucratic, top-down good-citizen model to a vibrant, collaborative, and inclusive system of leadership that reflects the values and vision of a new generation of young people. That system eschews the still-powerful star system that focuses on finding and supporting a handful of future leaders. In contrast, the new model assumes instead that all students, no matter how young or old, have a capacity to contribute to and participate in something larger than themselves.

This new concept of leadership requires a different kind of educational ethic. Traditionally, young people interested in becoming leaders were directed to the business or management schools, where they learned public speaking, goal setting, and budgeting. Now, as young people become more interested in leadership as public service, there must be new thinking about ways in which we educate and train for those positions, a point discussed later in Chapter 4.

Higher education is critical to this role. Colleges and universities act as gatekeepers into the world of social change and play a crucial role in shaping student attitudes about engagement of all kinds. But higher education too often views change as something students should do in their downtime, AmeriCorps as little more than a ticket to graduate school, and a life of service as a second-choice destination compared to the exhilarating, high-prestige jobs that once existed in the private sector.

Sixth, breakthrough does not occur by accident. Yes, luck happens. But luck is a faithless partner and often runs out. Social change requires strategy and a deep understanding of the complex economic, social, and political factors for creating impact. Political scientists often write about social breakthrough as a blend of four streams of inputs—policy entrepreneurs, ideas in good currency, problems and solutions, and opportunities for action.

The challenge is to cull these streams for opportunities to make a difference. Hence, political scientists also talk about legislative "freight trains" that provide opportunities for impact; "policy windows" that open for brief moments for action; and "punctuations" that occur in history when the prevailing wisdom becomes highly vulnerable. Notwithstanding this metaphor abuse, we must recognize that impact involves more than the power of a good idea—social breakthrough takes place in a political marketplace with its own dynamics. Bluntly put, good ideas cannot compel action without muscle.

What Readers Should Expect

Readers are forewarned that this book contains more questions than answers. We still have much to learn about challenging the prevailing wisdom and sustaining change, especially in a time of great political conflict. Campaign spending is expanding rapidly, social movements are exploding and collapsing on the right and left, and economic uncertainty has never been deeper.

Creating durable social change has never been easy—even a cursory review of the battle for civil rights, environmental protection, and human rights shows the risks ahead. But I cannot think of a more difficult moment in contemporary history to confront the prevailing wisdom. It is well financed, aggressive, and more than willing to distort the facts to its liking. Without the full engagement of every possible ally, breakthrough will remain well out of reach. And even when it occurs, it will not endure without highly motivated safekeepers, explorers, and advocates.

Social entrepreneurs can and often do play all of these roles, but might be infinitely faster to scale and achieve impact if they joined with others outside their community to create breakthrough networks. Not only do these networks aggregate enormous sum-greater-than-the-parts possibilities, but they also protect past breakthroughs from harm.

This is not a how-to book per se. Rather, it offers a series of ideas about how the change process works. Readers are encouraged to explore their own assumptions about key issues such as social entrepreneurship, other drivers of change, the stages that lead to breakthrough toward a new prevailing wisdom, and the central role that the infrastructure of change plays in assuring impact. There are recommendations along the way, but my primary goal is to set social entrepreneurship within the broader effort to address the urgent threats facing the world. Readers should bring their own opinions and experiences to these pages, and interpret, refine, expand, and even reject the overall conclusions. After all, this book reflects one author's journey, not absolute truth. It should be challenged just as rigorously as social entrepreneurs, safekeepers, explorers, and advocates challenge the prevailing wisdom about how to achieve change. As a social explorer, I bring a naturally contrarian nature to my task. In doing so, I hope to ignite a bit of disruption in the conversation. But my hope is to stimulate movement toward answering the fundamental question of this book: How do we solve the world's toughest problems? I believe the answer is "prepare to expect wonders."

Chapter 1

Still Searching for Social Entrepreneurship

Three decades after its first use, social entrepreneurship remains one of the most alluring terms on the problem-solving landscape and has even received a warm embrace from President Barack Obama. He stitched a variation of the concept into his 2009 Serve America Act, which simultaneously expanded Americorps and created a $50 million Social Innovation Fund. Obama has also created several national competitions to advance breakthroughs in education and health.

Obama clearly understands that the world faces a long list of urgent threats—poverty, hunger, disease, despair, pandemics, global climate change, aging economies, and so forth.

He also understands that the unthinkable is not only thinkable today but is approaching at light speed. His new Social Innovation Fund offers great promise for needed acceleration of social change, but is not enough for eventual success. Investors need to pour much more money into what works, and shut down programs that do not.

Obama is hardly the only national leader who understands the threats ahead. In 2009, for example, the Ford Foundation changed its logo and tagline to underscore a heightened focus on social breakthrough. Focusing on the "fierce urgency of now," the foundation's new tagline is simple: "Working with Visionaries on the Frontlines of Social Change Worldwide."

At first glance, the new logo and tagline embrace an exclusive definition of social entrepreneurship that favors individual action. After all, it focuses on visionaries as the source of breakthroughs in areas such as good governance, economic opportunity, better education, and freedom of expression. "We take enormous pride in our commitment to the visionary people who are seizing this moment and the promise it represents," the foundation's president, Luis A. Ubiñas, wrote. "With renewed focus and a shared optimism about what is possible, the Ford Foundation will be there to support them as they aspire to the fairness, freedom, opportunity, and dignity in which we all believe."

Yet, the logo and tagline also embrace an inclusive definition by focusing on the role of partnership and collaboration in creating social change. It does not define visionaries in the singular, for example, and includes organizations as a source of change. Even as the foundation focuses on the "people unafraid to take risks in search of lasting change," it is also clearly aware that these individuals do not work alone.

As such, the Ford Foundation's new logo and tagline blend the best of recent research on social entrepreneurship and breakthrough. The foundation's focus is on visionaries, but with a more inclusive approach to achieving solutions to the world's toughest problems. The foundation also clearly emphasizes the importance of aggregation to social impact. The search for new ideas is clear, but so is the need to move those ideas forward aggressively. As the foundation explains, civil society is essential for addressing complex and enduring problems. Without the organizations and partnerships to expand it, breakthrough seems impossible. The Ford Foundation's tagline is well worth copying.

The rest of this chapter deals with this changing definition of social entrepreneurship as a blend of both exclusive and inclusive approaches. The chapter begins with a discussion of divisions within the field, moves forward with a comparison of the exclusive and inclusive approaches, and addresses three questions that continue to bedevil the field. The basic definition and tactics underlying social entrepreneurship are changing quickly, and entrepreneurs and their funders confront new challenges in building lasting success.

It is important to note that social entrepreneurship will remain a field in flux for some time into the future. It is a new field ripe for further research, and the concept itself implies that there will be new combinations of ideas for basic definitions and learning. Social entrepreneurship is still inventing itself. Indeed, I would argue that social entrepreneurship must continue bending as it produces variation through its own exercise. This is not only healthy, but essential.

Building a Field

The Catherine B. Reynolds Foundation is just as committed as the Ford Foundation to building the field of social entrepreneurship through direct investment in developing new talent.

Although its budget is smaller than that of the Ford Foundation, the Reynolds effort is creating an enormous multiplier effect through a tight focus on preparing a new generation of social entrepreneurs for engagement.

The Reynolds Foundation is clearly committed to social change. Its vision statement declares: "The Catherine B. Reynolds Foundation strives to make a difference in its creative approach to philanthropy. It believes in direct action and creating powerful incentives that will stir young people to strive for excellence."

Like the Ford Foundation, the Reynolds Foundation believes in the power of individual imagination, which it supports through its annual Academy of Achievement. But it also believes in harnessing that imagination for the collective betterment of the world.

The Reynolds Foundation began investing in education for social entrepreneurship in 2005 with grants to Harvard University's John F. Kennedy School of Government and my home institution, New York University's Robert F. Wagner School of Public Service. These grants embrace an ecumenical approach too rarely applied in the field.

New York University now awards up to 10 undergraduate and 20 graduate fellowships annually to promising social entrepreneurs. The only catch is that no more than one-third of the fellows can come from any one of NYU's schools. Each class hails from every corner of the university, including our programs in business, public service, political science, social work, architecture, the arts, engineering, journalism, and the humanities.

The program covers a wide range of activities, including a speakers series and coaching sessions for each fellow. It also includes coursework in finance, business planning, social change, and project management, as well as a Leadership and

Social Transformation seminar that uses a blended definition of social entrepreneurship. The course description is clearly in sync with this book:

> The course explores the role of leadership in organizational efforts to change thinking, systems, and policies—taking into consideration the contested process by which the responsibility of addressing intractable problems is distributed among key diverse actors in a shared-power world. Traditional approaches to leadership defined by single heroic individuals who influence followers are contrasted with new perspectives—consistent with the demands of today's complex problems—particularly when we aspire to inclusive, transparent, and democratic solutions. Emergent perspectives reveal leadership as the collective achievement of members of a group who share a vision, and who must navigate the constellation of relationships, structures, processes, and institutional dynamics within the larger system in which they are embedded.

A Field Divided

The field of social entrepreneurship is still in its infancy. Research continues to lag action, definitions continue to evolve, and the knowledge base is fragmented. More troubling, the field still operates in silos of engagement in which partnerships are sometimes undervalued and collaboration lightly embraced. Instead of coming together as a field of both practice and research, social entrepreneurship is sometimes divided against itself. Consider the following list of challenges.

The definition of social entrepreneurship is changing rapidly as entrepreneurs and researchers work to create strategies for addressing urgent threats. David Bornstein and Susan Davis wrote about this evolution, *social entrepreneurship 3.0*, in their recent book *Social Entrepreneurship: What Everyone Needs to Know*:

> Social entrepreneurship 3.0 (today) looks beyond individual founders and institutions to change-making potential of *all* people and their interactions. It recognizes that social entrepreneurship is contagious. Every person who starts a social change organization emboldens others to pursue *their* ideas and solutions, whether by building institutions or by strengthening existing solutions through their investing, philanthropy, managing, advocacy, research, teaching, policy making, computer programming, purchasing, writing, and so forth.

Despite this emerging shift, the field of social entrepreneurship remains sharply divided between research and practice, as if research is somehow a drag on action. Although there is a growing body of research on social entrepreneurship, there is not enough interaction between lessons learned and new initiatives. Nor is there a significant effort to collect lessons learned across large samples of breakthroughs. Case studies do provide important insights on how social entrepreneurship works, but we have yet to build the large data sets that can reveal statistically significant findings.

The field is also sharply divided across academic disciplines and the professional schools that train social entrepreneurs. Even when the disciplines and schools are housed in the same buildings, they seem unable to communicate as they fight over ownership of the curricula. Social entrepreneurship has built a sometimes-tenuous relationship with business schools, for example, but has few connections with political science, public policy, social work, sociology, anthropology, philosophy, the humanities, and the hard sciences.

The field focuses almost exclusively on stories about lone wolves who struggle mightily against the odds to achieve impact, even though we now know that collaborative creativity may actually produce more success and fewer failures. The field has generally embraced a one-best-way approach to social change, meaning one hero, idea, organization, and strategy. But this one-best-way may be counter to the trial and error needed for true innovation.

The field has been less than enthusiastic about the need to develop clear theories of change and measuring results. Collaboration is clearly at the fore of the effort to replicate and scale social change, as it should be, but building successful social networks requires the same rigor that business entrepreneurs use to create the waves of creative destruction that knock out the prevailing wisdom (or at least displace it long enough to neutralize the old equilibrium that always lies in wait).

The field has yet to develop an inventory of entrepreneurial failure, even though there are obvious threats to survival as social entrepreneurs drive forward through the many obstacles they face. Success is obviously a great teacher, but control groups of missed opportunities are the coin of the realm for sorting the right lessons learned. We need to create inventories of what must go right *and* what cannot go wrong in conquering urgent threats.

The field sometimes dismisses the contributions of the large, old organizations that bring great experience and connections to social change. These so-called legacy organizations are often characterized as the last destination for innovation, a critique that denies the possibility that most organizations can innovate at moderate levels. The prevailing all-or-nothing wisdom about social entrepreneurship not only creates a singular focus on the individual, but also undermines partnerships with the many participants who contribute to breakthrough.

The field too often ignores the role of power in successful breakthroughs, perhaps because politics sometimes involves partisanship and hardball of the kind that produces congressional and/or media investigations. Yet, power is both part of the scale-up to breakthrough and a central driver in the social networks that aggregate pressure. As I argue later in this book, power, politics, and partisanship are either entirely missing from the dialogue about social entrepreneurship or hidden from view as a way to protect the field from attacks from the prevailing wisdom.

Finally, the field tends to minimize essential issues of organizational structure and management. Too many social entrepreneurs define management as drudgery—they want to imagine, invent, and dream, not raise money for heat, light, and computers. But poorly managed ideas are nearly impossible to scale to maximum impact whatever the tactic. And they are highly vulnerable to simple mistakes that can undermine momentum. Organization and management are too often confused with bureaucracy and red tape, even though business entrepreneurs know that effective management is essential to their ultimate success.

Many of these divisions are built around genuine excitement about the iconic entrepreneur. But this focus on the lone wolf has distracted the field from deeper conversations about building and maintaining the social breakthrough networks that have so often produced the great breakthroughs of the past. At least for now, we still tend to look for social entrepreneurship in one sector (nonprofit), driven by one person (the entrepreneur), with an unusually focused set of skills and motivations (what venture capital firm Ashoka's Bill Drayton calls the entrepreneurial quality), operating in a special setting (almost always new and mostly young).

A Field Uniting

Despite these divisions, the field of social entrepreneurship is also coming together in important ways, not the least of which involves a growing concern for collaboration and focused advocacy. Consider the following list of gains.

The field contains individual entrepreneurs such as Billy Shore of Share Our Strength, Dr. Paul Farmer of Partners in Health, and Ami Dar of idealist.org (who would never call himself a social entrepreneur) who have demonstrated enormous courage, inspiration, passion, and perseverance toward measurable social impact, while acknowledging that they cannot succeed alone.

The field also contains individual scholars such as J. Gregory Dees, Johanna Mair, Jane Wei-Skillern, Alex Nicholls, Paul Bloom, and Christine Letts who are drilling deeply into the basic concept of social entrepreneurship, looking for patterns that might explain success and reduce failure. Although they are motivated by the hope for impact, we are all contrarians of a sort—we must challenge the conventional wisdom of social entrepreneurship, just as social entrepreneurship challenges the conventional wisdom about social threats.

The field has created new opportunities to share research emerging across the world, most notably the biannual Colloquium on Social Entrepreneurship co-hosted by Duke University's Center for the Advancement of Social Entrepreneurship and Oxford University's Skoll Center for Social

Entrepreneurship. The three-day annual colloquium was first convened with a handful of scholars and a modest list of panels in 2008, but had expanded to dozens of researchers and a deep inventory of papers by 2010.

The field is now supported by funders such as the Acumen Fund, the Edna McConnell Clark Foundation, REDF (formerly the Roberts Enterprise Development Fund), and the Robert Wood Johnson Foundation committed to proven concepts and the infrastructure to attain success, and other organizations such as the Nonprofit Finance Fund that are committed to infrastructure support. And there is a growing sense in Washington, D.C., that scale-up is an essential act for both new combinations of ideas and highly effective programs already on the books.

The field now has sources of venture capital such as Ashoka, Echoing Green, and New Profit, Inc., that can provide the kick-start toward invention and scale-up; there are also giant organizations such as the Gates, Ford, and Rockefeller foundations that are putting up substantial sums to generate deep social impact, as well as small foundations such as the F.B. Heron Foundation that are investing substantial portions of their endowments in social engagement.

The field is also investing in studying urgent threats through think tanks, such as the Skoll Foundation's Urgent Threats Fund, that are analyzing and monitoring trends that might reveal oncoming tipping points. Its first two grants went to an organization called J Street to elevate the voices of moderation toward Middle East peace, and the Ploughshares Fund to foster support for a world completely free of nuclear weapons. There are also funders such as the Gates, Hewlett, and Packard foundations that are investing in measurable results while addressing similar urgent threats.

The field also contains social entrepreneurs who are now asking how to create collective impact through social networks such as the Campaign for Tobacco-Free Kids that have shown significant success in driving policy change. These partnerships are part of the new research and collaboration promoted by new practice networks such as Duke's Center for Social Impact, which is led by Edward Skloot, former head of the Surdna Foundation and one of the first to use the term *social entrepreneurship*.

There are many programs that are scaling to impact in aggressive partnership with national programs such as the U.S. Department of Education's Race to the Top. Although it has been controversial, the Race to the Top put $4.5 billion at risk for encouraging innovative school reform (Delaware and Tennessee won the first round).

Led in large part by New Leaders for New Schools, the Race was the product of a broad alliance of social entrepreneurs and advocates. Regardless of whether one agrees with the effort to create stronger ties between teacher performance and pay, the alliance has produced major policy changes across the states, including legislation to raise arbitrary caps on the number of charter schools. "This is not heavy-handed Washington command-and-control," *New York Times* columnist David Brooks wrote on June 6, 2010. "This is Washington energizing diverse communities of reformers, locality by locality, and giving them more leverage in their struggles against the defenders of the prevailing wisdom."

The field is broadening to include corporate social ventures such as TOMS Shoes and the Greyston Bakery (think chocolate fudge brownie ice cream) that make a profit in pursuit of social impact; in fact, *BusinessWeek* now publishes an annual list of the most effective social-venture firms, including Books for Good, which resells used books around the world. These firms make profits by producing social impact, which is one way to reduce the dependency on funders who sometimes put their own interests in claiming credit ahead of durable support.

At the same time, many corporations are adopting genuine principles for guiding ethical profit making. These firms do not use social responsibility as a clever marketing tool, but as part of double- and triple-bottom lines that measure their financial, environmental, and social impact. They are key participants in erasing the artificial barriers between business and social change. Instead of using social responsibility to "greenwash" dismal social records, these authentic firms are willing to sacrifice small margins of profit in working toward reducing inequality, intolerance, environmental abuse, unemployment, the use of child labor, and discrimination.

Finally, there are private firms that are creating highly profitable and world-changing innovations toward a new social equilibrium. *New York Times* columnist Thomas Friedman celebrated several of these firms in his March 7, 2010, contribution. Writing about SunPower and Bloom Energy, Friedman noted the global value of business entrepreneurship in creating cleaner, low-cost energy. Not only are such firms able to raise more flexible capital than most nonprofits, including the new *low-profit limited liability companies (L3Cs)* that are starting to spring up, but they also seem to have faster idea-to-market success.

As this list suggests, there is a growing effort to bridge the divisions both within the field of social entrepreneurship and with other actors in the social-change cycle. In fact, the challenge may not be too little sparking, but too much isolation. There are very real incentives for staying separate, avoiding mergers and acquisitions, creating proprietary projects, and keeping secrets. This may make perfect sense for becoming *the* one place to go for social impact, but can be self-defeating nonetheless. Distinctiveness and exclusiveness do little to increase the odds of social change.

Defining Terms

Much as the field agrees that social entrepreneurship involves the pursuit of a new equilibrium, we still have work to do in defining how to sweep away the prevailing wisdom and create sustainable social breakthrough in its place. Some definitions offer a more inclusive definition of social entrepreneurship, while others are singularly focused.

The choice of an inclusive or exclusive definition has obvious implications for making choices on how to create social breakthrough, not the least of which involves investment by governments, other funders, nonprofit organizations, businesses, interest groups, and so forth. Should we favor the individual entrepreneur, look for teams and the collaborative creativity they energize, or seek a mix of both?

An Inclusive Definition

My own work on social entrepreneurship began with a set of challenges that were published in my 2006 article "Reshaping Social Entrepreneurship." My question at the time was not at all whether social entrepreneurs exist—that much was certain in the most cursory sampling of the Ashoka, Echoing Green, and Skoll Foundation award winners from recent years.

Rather, I argued that the field might be too exclusive for its own good. By defining social entrepreneurship more by the characteristics of the individual entrepreneurs who forge social value through their work, I wrote, "the field may have excluded large numbers of individuals and entities that are equally deserving of the support, networking, and training now reserved for individuals who meet both the current definitional tests of a social entrepreneur and the ever-growing list of exemplars."

Hence, my 2006 definition of social entrepreneurship was much more inclusive than the prevailing wisdom that exists in the field:

> Social entrepreneurship is an effort by an individual, group, network, organization, or alliance of organizations that seeks sustainable, large-scale impact through pattern-breaking ideas in what governments, nonprofits, and businesses do to address significant social problems.

Having sorted hundreds of articles on social and business entrepreneurship between 2006 and 2008, I came to a much crisper definition in my 2008 book, *The Search for Social Entrepreneurship:*

> Social entrepreneurship is an effort to solve an intractable social problem through pattern-breaking change.

Social entrepreneurship is no doubt courageous, authentic, and often successful in challenging the prevailing wisdom, but it is best viewed as one of several drivers of change nonetheless. It is a means to an end.

Moreover, social entrepreneurship is not always a full-time organizational activity. Some individuals and organizations may be highly entrepreneurial most of the time, others highly entrepreneurial only some of the time, still others moderately entrepreneurial all of the time, and so forth. It is not clear, however, just which level of engagement is the most productive for social breakthrough. Much as we celebrate 24/7 entrepreneurs, it may be that the most promising ideas arise from rather ordinary people with extraordinary vision. It is the idea, not the level of activity, that matters.

As such, I believe that the amount of social entrepreneurship can be increased by supporting more potential entrepreneurs as they cross over to public leadership at any point in life, from any sector, with any history, and at high, moderate, or even relatively low levels of production. Given my notion that established organizations are perfectly capable of producing social entrepreneurship, many social entrepreneurs are hidden from view, and some adamantly refuse to use the term. These social entrepreneurs may be buried within their organizations, but their social breakthroughs can be found in the innovations that occur on the front lines, sometimes without the slightest permission from above.

An Exclusive Alternative

My 2006 definition of social entrepreneurship provoked an intense reaction within the field, especially surrounding my notion that social entrepreneurs might not be as rare as imagined. In questioning the focus on individuals, I had mistakenly implied that lone wolves were somehow unimportant to social entrepreneurship.

Ashoka's Bill Drayton put this notion to rest in an emphatic letter to the *Stanford Social Innovation Review* in 2007. Social entrepreneurship comes from the individual, he wrote, in part because each individual is unique: "Leading social entrepreneurs are remarkable. They are doing something enormously important and difficult—something that in many ways is critical for society and, in its nature, demands much of an entrepreneur's life. These strong and often lonely human beings require and deserve our long-term understanding, loyalty, and respect."

Drayton also argued that social entrepreneurs follow a well-worn path into engagement: "Entrepreneurs capable of making profound pattern changes are rare and have a well-understood and strikingly coherent, consistent life history. After a long apprenticeship in established institutions, there comes a time when the entrepreneur is no longer able to grow or move his or her ideas ahead. In most cases, he or she must build new institutions to serve an idea that cuts across the old organizational lines, thought patterns, and disciplines."

Translated in arguably simplistic terms, social entrepreneurs take frustrating jobs, become agitated with the lack of opportunities to make a difference, exit their organizations, and start their own ventures, often without a clue about potential support.

Past research strongly suggests that Drayton was mostly right in his two-pronged critique.

First, there is no doubt that there are successful lone wolves at work on social change—just visit www.skollfoundation.org and scroll down its list of award winners. At the same time, there are also teams, partnerships, families, organizational employees, and even communities that produce social entrepreneurship.

Second, the research suggests that many social entrepreneurs share similar histories. There is growing evidence that most social entrepreneurs start their efforts in the same city and same field where they began their careers, and often use the same networks and the same skills. They either are forced to make the leap because they lose their jobs or choose to leave because of frustration and dead ends. They see an opportunity to create something of their own, and they take it.

There were other defenses of exclusiveness in the wake of my article, including a tough critique by Roger Martin and Sally Osberg. Writing in the spring 2007 issue of the *Stanford Social Innovation Review*, they argued that social entrepreneurship should not be used to describe "all manner of socially beneficial activities." Although Martin and Osberg made the case that inclusiveness could be a good thing, especially if plenty of resources are flowing into the field, it dilutes focus during scarcity. "Because of this danger," the authors argued, "we believe that we need a much sharper definition of social entrepreneurship, one that enables us to determine the extent to which an activity is and is not 'in the tent.'"

Martin and Osberg took an important step toward that sharper definition by defining social entrepreneurship as a successful effort to alter the social equilibrium, which I tend to imagine as a dense cloud filled with policies (products), citizens (consumers), organizations (firms), and so forth—or even the night lights of the aurora borealis.

According to Martin and Osberg, social entrepreneurship starts with "an unfortunate but stable equilibrium that causes the exclusion, neglect, marginalization, or suffering of a segment of humanity"; which engages an individual "who brings to bear on this situation his or her inspiration, direct action, creativity, courage, and fortitude"; which creates a "new stable equilibrium that secures permanent benefits for the targeted group and society at large."

This choice of words drew a heavy assist from the work of Austrian economist Joseph Schumpeter, who described business entrepreneurship as a form of "creative destruction" that permanently disturbs the prevailing business equilibrium. As such, the article provided momentum toward a more precise definition of impact. But Martin and Osberg's definition still leaves plenty of room for further debate about what kinds of activities actually constitute social entrepreneurship, a debate that Martin and Osberg engaged by arguing that social services and advocacy can coexist with social entrepreneurship in hybrid forms but should not be mixed into the inclusive definition of the term.

Sorting Assumptions

Much as I admire Martin and Osberg's search for definitional clarity, the following distinction between "rigorous" and "inclusive" creates more heat than light. "If we can achieve a rigorous definition," Martin and Osberg wrote, "then those who support social entrepreneurship can focus their resources on building and strengthening a concrete and identifiable field. Absent that discipline, proponents of social entrepreneurship run the risk of giving the skeptics an ever-expanding target to shoot at, and the cynics even more reason to discount social innovation and those who drive it."

Given my past work, it is no surprise that I might believe an inclusive definition can be quite rigorous, even as an exclusive definition can be based more on casual observation than evidence. In fact, rigor and breadth actually involve two very different variables that cannot be combined into a single continuum. Simply put, definitions can be both inclusive *and* valid and exclusive *but* invalid.

Table 1.1 provides a framework for sorting the many hypotheses about each, along with several examples. Rigor depends on evidence-based research, not the effort to winnow potential grantees by avoiding tough choices based on their own integrity, honesty, trust, and faith. It is absolute nonsense to argue otherwise by creating a definitional continuum anchored by "inclusiveness" at one end and "rigor" at the other.

Despite the need for more evidence, there has been a sharp decline in funding for social entrepreneurship research on these kinds of questions. Stretched to their limits by the recession,

Table 1.1 Sorting Assumptions

	Inclusive	**Exclusive**
Rigorous and verified	Social entrepreneurs can be individuals, teams, groups, communities, and so forth.	Social entrepreneurs need a set of specific, identifiable, and distinctive skills to succeed.
Asserted but not verified	Social entrepreneurs are born, not made.	Social entrepreneurs are different from other high achievers.

many foundations are withdrawing from research altogether, thereby increasing the likelihood of serious errors in selecting the most effective interventions. Some errors involve rejecting a true hypothesis without proof, while others involve accepting a false hypothesis on the basis of hunch.

I have committed both statistical errors in my research on social entrepreneurship—errors that I corrected as I searched for evidence to support or deny specific assertions about entrepreneurs, ideas, opportunities, and organizations. I am not done with this work, but do recognize that all of us carry untested notions about our definitions—for example, that social entrepreneurs must work 24/7 to succeed. Although these intensely committed individuals are certainly alluring, there is little evidence that sleep deprivation, emotional and physical stress, and social isolation are essential ingredients of success. Quite the contrary; overworked entrepreneurs often make their greatest mistakes when they put their work ahead of personal health.

A Blended Definition of Social Entrepreneurship

A more inclusive definition of social entrepreneurship produces an immediate result: Social entrepreneurship can be found almost everywhere. Although award and fellowship programs might yield long lists of names and organizations for possible study, such lists would not contain the sometime-entrepreneurs or on-hold entrepreneurs out there. Similarly, case studies might miss the once-moribund organizations that have suddenly rediscovered themselves, or the self-effacing, non-media-savvy entrepreneurs who prefer to remain anonymous.

Instead of searching for the proverbial needle in the haystack, I believe that there are needles almost everywhere, thereby raising hopes there are more social entrepreneurs the field has yet to discover. Some of these entrepreneurs may need little more than a push to make the leap of faith toward social breakthrough. Others may need a more substantial boost in visibility and financial support to move through scale-up and sustained results. Still others may be doing well as they are.

The challenge is to avoid assumptions that reduce social entrepreneurship to just another term that gets bandied about in funding proposals and niche competitions. Other terms, such as innovation, have gone that route and may never be rescued from overuse. At the same time, social entrepreneurship should not be defined so narrowly that it becomes the province of the special few who crowd out potential support and assistance for individuals and entities that are just as special but less well-known.

In the end, the research goal should be to uncover the factors that make all forms of social agitation successful. If these factors suggest that social entrepreneurs must suffer to succeed, so be it. At least the conclusion would yield insights on how to make the struggle easier. If, however, the research suggests that social entrepreneurs can produce change through a more natural process, even better.

Even though I have moved toward a more exclusive definition of social entrepreneurship over the past four years, I still remain an outlier in the field, in part because of persistent questions about three of the most important assumptions: Must social entrepreneurs always invent alone? Are they truly different from other high achievers? And are there different kinds of social entrepreneurship?

Must Social Entrepreneurs Invent Alone?

Funders often deify the heroes who create new combinations of ideas late at night in their basement studies, I remain convinced that lone wolves are just one source of social entrepreneurship. This is not to suggest that individual heroes do not exist. Nor is it to argue that the spark of imagination always occurs collectively. Rather, it is to confront the notion that collections of individuals are somehow a poor substitute for brilliant solo artists.

To the contrary, even as we rightly celebrate the heroic individuals who have committed their lives to social breakthrough, the research suggests that collaboration is an equal, if not always preferred, tactic for producing the equilibrium-changing ideas. Collaborative creativity, as it is sometimes called, is a powerful tool for increasing the odds of success and trimming the incidence of failures.

Consider the findings from a recent study of more than 500,000 U.S. patents, which is a sound measure of business innovation. According to the study, innovative teams both *inside* and *outside* larger organizations have not only a higher percentage of successes (defined as patentable innovations), but a lower percentage of failures. They are better at (1) finding new combinations of ideas, (2) selecting successful proposals, and (3) rejecting potential failures. Indeed, teams are not only more effective than the classic garage innovator celebrated in Western culture, but they are also more effective than the so-called mad scientist who works alone within an oppressive organization.

Jasjit Singh and Lee Fleming described the pattern in a January 2010 *Management Science* article. Asking whether the lone inventor is more or less likely to invent breakthroughs, they use 500,000 patents to establish that lone wolves are less likely to innovate outside of where they work. Singh and Fleming conclude that "those who work alone and outside of an organization are least likely of all to invent a breakthrough."

Their summary of the role of teams is well worth reading in its entirety.

> Teams have an inherent advantage in the identification of the best ideas. A collaborative team will consider the invention from a greater variety of viewpoints and potential applications; such broader consideration is more likely to uncover problems. Given the typically greater diversity of experience on a collaborative team, some member is more likely to recall having seen a problem with a similar invention and argue to abandon or modify the approach.
>
> In short, collaborative creativity will subject individually conceived ideas to a more rigorous selection process so that fewer poor ideas are pursued. Independent of the idea's source (lone versus collaborative), we propose that collaboration improves the effectiveness of the selection phase because collaborative selection will be more rigorous than lone selection.

Translated into baseball terms, collaborative creativity produces more hits, steals, extra bases, runs, and home runs, even as it also produces fewer errors, strikeouts, missed signals, and runners left on base.

As Singh and Fleming also show, even collaborative creativity located within a large organization produces better results than lone-wolf innovation:

> Arguments similar to benefits from affiliation with teams can also be made for affiliation with organizations. We propose that a single independent inventor (the image here is of an antisocial individual working in his or her garage) will be more isolated than a single inventor who works within an organization. The assumption is that an affiliated inventor who does not collaborate will still enjoy more social interaction (among colleagues and technical experts) than an unaffiliated inventor. This assumption is consistent with perspectives that the ability to accumulate and leverage knowledge provides a key reason for the existence of firms. Accordingly, firms can be seen as social communities that are a natural extension of teams when it comes to creation of new knowledge. Though there are surely exceptions of highly connected yet independent inventors, our argument depends on the typical independent inventor being more isolated than the typical affiliated inventor. Because isolated inventors will lack multiple and (to varying degrees) uncorrelated filters, they will uncover fewer potential problems and hence develop more dead ends.

Notwithstanding this growing body of evidence on the power of collaboration, the field of social entrepreneurship still focuses primarily on lone wolves. It often seems that the more isolated the entrepreneur, the more likely the funding.

The field is starting to embrace the collaborative model, however. Bill Drayton made this point in his April 8, 2010, contribution to McKinsey & Company's What Matters web site. Although he clearly believes that lone wolves matter greatly to social change, his Ashoka fellows are increasingly working together to forge large coalitions for change:

> Over the last half-dozen years we have been developing something with even more far-reaching impact—*collaborative entrepreneurship*. There has never been anything like it before. However, once there are several hundred leading social entrepreneurs in a field across the continents, one can be confident that a jump to the next paradigm in the field is near. . . . Once it is thus clear where the world must go, the community then determines what one or two things must happen if the world is to get there—and somewhere between a third and a half of the leading social entrepreneur Fellows then work together to tip the seven to ten countries that are critical ultimately to tipping the world.

The same can be said of the individuals and teams that unite to create a new combination in the first place. The field of social entrepreneurship is clearly moving now toward collaborative teams, albeit ones composed of social entrepreneurs who have already created their own initiatives. It cannot be long before the concept expands to teams of all potential players in creating breakthroughs.

Are Social Entrepreneurs Truly Different?

Even as the field moves toward a more inclusive definition of social entrepreneurship by embracing collaboration, there is still an underlying belief that social entrepreneurs are somehow different from other entrepreneurs in the worlds of business, arts, sciences, and so forth. No matter how and where they create their ideas, whether as lone wolves or in large teams, in their basements or in large organizations, are social entrepreneurs truly a rare breed?

At the start of my research journey in 2006, I challenged the notion that social entrepreneurs were different from other entrepreneurs and high achievers in general. Like other entrepreneurs, they believe in a more hopeful future and are driven by a persistent, almost unshakable optimism. Like other entrepreneurs, they also persevere in large part because they believe they will not fail.

By 2008, however, I had changed my assumption to a more exclusive approach. I came to believe that social entrepreneurs are very different from other entrepreneurs in their deep commitment to address social injustice. Unlike business entrepreneurs, who pursue new ideas for profit and glory, social entrepreneurs are clearly motivated by the desire to help others. Although some social entrepreneurs also make profits through social ventures, and others seem to seek glory, social entrepreneurs are not mere billiard balls deflected by accident into the social breakthrough pocket. Rather, they are motivated by a sense of social injustice that other entrepreneurs do not have.

At the same time, there is mixed evidence at best that entrepreneurs of any kind are really that different from high achievers in general. As William Gartner wrote in his seminal 1988 article, "Entrepreneurs often *do* seem like special people who achieve things that most of us do not achieve. These achievements, we think, must be based on some special inner quality. It is difficult *not* to think this way."

However, Gartner could find little evidence to support this image. Describing his search for "this entity known as the entrepreneur," Gartner concluded that personality characteristics were "ancillary" to entrepreneurial behavior: "Research on the entrepreneur should focus on what the entrepreneur does and not who the entrepreneur is." Twenty years and hundreds of studies later, Gartner's conclusion remains unchallenged.

Despite this evidence, the field is moving toward a blended position on this key assumption. Yes, social entrepreneurs have different goals and perhaps more traumatic childhoods than business entrepreneurs, but no, there is little research that suggests these differences are especially important to their success.

It is safest therefore to suggest that social entrepreneurs are more than another breed of business entrepreneur. They have very different destinations in life and less interest in making money. They make embrace businesslike thinking, but only to the extent it drives their social agendas.

Are There Different Kinds of Social Entrepreneurship?

The search for social entrepreneurship may be missing the forest for the definitional trees. It is quite possible that Martin and Osberg are defining just one type of social entrepreneurship, while I am describing another. Perhaps lone wolves are particularly useful in creating those legions of imitators or at early moments of the impact effort when hope seems lost. Perhaps collaborations are more effective in massing for policy impact or at later steps of the impact process when momentum is essential.

Consider for a moment at least two somewhat different types of social entrepreneurs, each of which has a role to play in social change. Table 1.2 provides some speculative

Table 1.2 A Speculative Comparison of Type A and Type B Social Entrepreneurship

	Type A Social Entrepreneurship	**Type B Social Entrepreneurship**
Entrepreneur: Who does the work?	Lone wolf driven 24/7 passion Higher demand for consensus Higher focus on visibility Higher optimism about success	Team driven Lower intensity Higher tolerance of dissent Lower focus on visibility Higher concerns about failure
Idea: What do entrepreneurs produce?	Higher focus on program innovation High risk tolerance Higher focus on distinctiveness Lower interest in fine-tuning More intuitiveness	Higher focus on process innovation Less risk tolerance Higher focus on experimentation Higher competition among ideas More long-range planning
Opportunity: When do entrepreneurs act?	Higher focus on creating new opportunity Higher need for alertness Higher "David" orientation Greater certainty of success Funded externally	Higher focus on exploiting existing opportunity Higher need for agility Higher "sure thing" orientation More second-guessing Funded internally
Organization: Where do entrepreneurs work?	More multitasking Flatter hierarchy Less participation Younger, smaller Weaker governance	More specialization Thicker hierarchy More delegation Older, larger More red tape
Social impact: What is the bottom line?	Fewer successes Faster implementation Greatest threats come from outside the organization Potential founder's syndrome Fewer partnerships, greater focus on proprietary protection	Fewer failures Slower implementation Greatest threats come from inside the organization Potential orphan ideas More partnerships, less focus on protection

comparisons of what might be called Type A and Type B social entrepreneurship.

Type A

My definition of Type A social entrepreneurship is built upon Martin and Osberg's work—the lone wolf, 24/7 passions, unrelenting optimism, a new organization, and an unshakable commitment to change. Type A entrepreneurs appear to be Type A personalities, meaning they are absolutely and passionately committed to whatever-it-takes change. Their faith in the possible can produce overconfidence, a certain degree of hubris, and an unwillingness to confront potential weaknesses in their plans. They appear to be highly motivated by achievement and possibly more intuitive in choosing drivers toward impact, which exposes them to greater risks of failure.

Driven by their early experiences in life, they persevere against the odds, and may even find greater energy as the conventional wisdom pushes back. They may be more intuitive than Type B entrepreneurs, meaning that they are more likely to be dreamers than scientists, more likely to be inspired by the creative process than by market pressure. In short, they may act out of a very deep concern for curing injustice rather than the need to create new combinations as a way to meet organizational pressure.

Even as they harness their personal passion, Type A entrepreneurs may find it difficult to work with others in their effort even to the point of discouraging dissent within their own organizations. They also appear to struggle with governance and accounting issues and may have greater difficulty measuring pace and impacts. Their organizations appear to be more agile and alert in many ways, but they may be unable to bring resources to bear on potential opportunities, in part because they operate so close to the financial margin. Their greatest vulnerabilities involve a lack of basic organizational capacity, which may reflect the lack of unrestricted and diversified revenues.

Type B

Type B social entrepreneurship is perhaps best described by the moderately entrepreneurial organizations that I found among the social-change organizations I surveyed for *The Search for Social Entrepreneurship*. The moderately entrepreneurial organizations clearly had the capacity for social breakthrough, but also had some of the bureaucratic weight that makes such activity more difficult.

There were times when the moderately entrepreneurial organizations looked more like highly entrepreneurial organizations compared with their not-too-entrepreneurial peers. For example, respondents at the moderately entrepreneurial organizations reported much higher levels of founder involvement, higher overall performance, and a somewhat lower commitment to being well managed than their not-too-entrepreneurial peers reported.

There were other times, however, when the moderately entrepreneurial organizations looked exactly like their not-too-entrepreneurial peers. For example, respondents at my moderately entrepreneurial organizations reported similar budget growth, demand for services, external vulnerability, and the lack of basic resources such as information technology and training.

Either way, my research suggests social entrepreneurship is not always a 24/7 activity and most certainly not an all-consuming organizational passion. New combinations can arise through chance encounters with reality, and can be stimulated by idea generators such as suggestion programs and internal venture competitions. Instead of the star systems that favor the charismatic inventors, my moderately entrepreneurial organizations allowed innovation to spring from any corner.

Moderately entrepreneurial organizations also reported the greatest diversification of programs and funding as well as the largest budgets among the three groups of social benefit organizations. Although diversification is not a panacea for all that ails nonprofit organizations, it can provide occasional opportunities for investment in social entrepreneurship. Facing slower growth, though growth nonetheless, these moderately entrepreneurial organizations may have used diversification to subsidize their pattern-breaking impact.

Choosing Types

These comparisons between Type A and Type B entrepreneurship are still speculative, but each type appears in the literature on social change. It could be that Type A entrepreneurship is the best driver for program innovation, while Type B is the better driver for fine-tuning and process improvement. Nevertheless, the comparisons do underscore the notion that social entrepreneurship is not a one-size-fits-all phenomenon. The two types are not either-or, but rather both-and.

J. Gregory Dees was right in 1998 when he described social entrepreneurship as an exceptional act by exceptional people, whatever the entrepreneurial type. He advised, "These behaviors should be encouraged and rewarded in those who have the capabilities and temperament for this kind of work. We could use many more of them." But as Dees cautioned, not everyone is well suited to entrepreneurship: "Social entrepreneurs are one special breed of leader, and they should be recognized as such. This definition preserves their distinctive status and assures that social entrepreneurship is not treated lightly. We need social entrepreneurs to help us find new avenues toward social improvement as we enter the next century."

Although there may be much more social entrepreneurship across the sectors than previously imagined, success still involves a struggle against an entrenched equilibrium that often denies simple common sense. Indeed, if I had to pick one core characteristic of successful social entrepreneurs beyond commitment to vision, it would be perseverance against an array of obstacles, a point well made by Dees in arguing that social entrepreneurs act boldly without regard to resources in hand. This perseverance can exist in lone wolves and teams, in an individual's personal hubris and a well-funded idea incubator, and in new and old organizations. We need to move away from the old one-best-way approach to building high-performance entrepreneurship and toward a more ecumenical approach.

This embrace of a broader image of the entrepreneur as both a singular and a plural term suggests that the number of social entrepreneurs is neither small nor static. Drayton may be quite right that the number of potential social entrepreneurs is quite low (perhaps just 1 in 10 million). But there is considerable research that suggests we can generate more social entrepreneurship through education, training, and encouragement. The federal government has a host of programs for increasing the number of business entrepreneurs, for example, not to mention whole departments and agencies, while the Ewing Marion Kauffman Foundation has embarked on an ambitious effort to strengthen entrepreneurship education at the nation's business schools. Perhaps a similar focus on potential social entrepreneurs might work just as well.

A New Inventory of Assumptions

As the research on social entrepreneurship continues to grow, the field must confront its own prevailing wisdom about how breakthroughs occur. This prevailing wisdom is particularly powerful in shaping investment decisions of all kinds—fellowships for individual entrepreneurs, grants for growth, signals to government grant programs such as the federal government's Social Innovation Fund. If social entrepreneurship comes in many sizes and shapes, investors must be much more flexible in their own prevailing wisdom about how change occurs. They must hedge against their own bias in focusing on exclusivity. As Table 1.3 suggests, the prevailing wisdom about social entrepreneurship is built on a series of increasingly questionable assumptions.

Table 1.3 Alternative Assumptions about Social Entrepreneurship

Prevailing Wisdom	Amended Prevailing Wisdom
Entrepreneurs	
Lone wolves are the primary source of social change.	FALSE—Social entrepreneurs also work in collaborative teams.
Social entrepreneurs share very similar strategies.	FALSE—There are different kinds of social entrepreneurship.
Social entrepreneurs are different from other high achievers.	FALSE—Social entrepreneurs may have a different purpose, but share many similar skills.
Ideas	
New combinations of ideas are essential for social change.	FALSE—Breakthroughs often occur through the expansion of old ideas.
Initial testing of new combinations is often a distraction from scaling.	FALSE—Research and development spending is a particularly powerful but often neglected investment strategy.
Breakthroughs are usually surprising and novel.	FALSE—Breakthroughs often involve new combinations of familiar ideas.

Opportunities	
Opportunities are discovered, not created.	FALSE—Opportunities can be created through agitation and advocacy.
Opportunities arise at essentially random intervals.	FALSE—Opportunities often arise in waves during relatively brief punctuations in history.
Opportunities reveal themselves to a special few.	FALSE—Opportunities can be widely identified and disseminated through trend analysis.
Organizations	
Social entrepreneurship thrives in flat and porous organizations.	FALSE—Social entrepreneurs can emerge in highly bureaucratic settings, albeit at greater cost.
Social entrepreneurship requires new and young organizations.	FALSE—Established organizations can and do produce breakthroughs, and often have the dissemination networks for rapid scaling.
Organizational growth is essential for success.	FALSE—Impact, not rapid growth, is the key measure of success.
Social Impact	
Social entrepreneurship destroys the prevailing wisdom.	FALSE—The prevailing wisdom is rarely destroyed.
Social entrepreneurship advances almost entirely through replication and imitation.	FALSE—Breakthroughs also occur through policy changes that mandate change through regulation.
Social entrepreneurship demands proprietary protection.	FALSE—Breakthroughs involve collaboration and information sharing.

The prevailing wisdom about social entrepreneurship is shifting quickly toward this more ecumenical approach. Investors such as the Skoll Foundation are moving toward the center of what will be labeled "social entrepreneurship 4.0" relatively soon, while lone wolves are moving slowly toward the periphery as the best alternative for change.

This is not to denigrate heroes, of course. They will always play a key role in the breakthrough networks that aggregate pressure. But the current prevailing wisdom has focused on heroes as an almost exclusive source of lessons learned. The search for an exclusive definition of social entrepreneurship will no doubt continue—that is how academic fields are built. But this search for exclusivity can become a barrier to the thoughtful investing it seeks. The focus should be on creating as much entrepreneurship as possible through every means available, including efforts to raise the number of social entrepreneurs.

Moreover, the field must be more careful about defining social entrepreneurship as just another form of business entrepreneurship. Business entrepreneurship offers many important lessons for solving seemingly intractable problems, not the least of which is the role of imagination, invention, research and development, and launch in eventual breakthroughs.

However, the analogy between business and social entrepreneurship can be stretched too far. Perhaps Harvard University professor Graham T. Allison Jr. would agree. Writing in 1979 on government and private management, he asked whether the two were "fundamentally alike in all unimportant respects." Although he found significant overlap between the two sectors on general strategy, production, and marketing, he wondered how much further the learning might go. According to Allison, government can learn a great deal from business about how to deliver services, whereas business has less to say about who gets what, when, and where in the great battles ahead.

Allison might apply the same logic to business and social entrepreneurship: Are they also fundamentally alike in all unimportant respects? Business and social entrepreneurship both create waves of creative destruction, for example, but the destruction is not the same. When the waves crash ashore in business, whole industries are washed away for good. When the waves come ashore in social entrepreneurship, however, the industries of deprivation rarely disappear. Having reaped the profits of deprivation through poverty, disease, environmental degradation, and injustice, they fight hard to regain power and reverse change. They are not known as defenders of the prevailing wisdom for nothing—they prevail through the blunt exercise of power and control, crushing breakthroughs by every means at their disposal.

A Lingering Question

A blended definition of social entrepreneurship accepts the notion that entrepreneurs bring a special set of skills and motivations to their work. They may or may not be different from other high achievers, but they are high achievers nonetheless. Thus, one of the most important questions for future research and funding involves the key assets of successful social entrepreneurs. Simply asked, what do successful change agents need?

Answering this question is essential for expanding the pipeline of future change agents, but must involve much greater rigor toward developing what the Echoing Green Foundation is now calling the *social entrepreneurship quotient (SEQ)*. Echoing Green readily admits that its SEQ is a work in progress, but the inventory nonetheless represents a very serious effort to pin down the personal foundations of successful change. It also addresses the need for some kind of evidence-based tool for moving past the "we know it when we see it" inventories of individual and team commitment toward a more sophisticated sorting of what does and does not matter for actual success.

This is a critically important effort for the field, if only because it shapes basic investment decisions—who should be funded, what skills social entrepreneurs need, what makes them successful, what can and cannot be taught, who gets into the figurative tent, and who should be discouraged from further action.

Past research on business entrepreneurs has produced at least one agreement and one caveat that are relevant to the search. The agreement focuses on the nature of the entrepreneur as an unconventional thinker. Focusing on scientific breakthroughs in her 1995 study, Carol Steiner identified practicality, authenticity/creativity, and teamwork as the three markers of unconventional thinking among scientists and engineers. For Steiner, science is a necessary component of the innovative idea. "Yet innovation needs visionaries able to take in the big picture. It needs individuals confident enough to shake off the straitjacket of specialist paradigms. Most of all, it needs free agents to creatively and individually interpret a complex world through a complicated interpersonal process."

The caveat involves the lack of hard evidence to make this case. Virtually every recent article on underlying personality differences ends with a call for more research. "What lies beneath?" Norris Krueger Jr. asked in the title of his 2007 article. "The experiential essence of entrepreneurial thinking," he answered. But having summarized the best available evidence, Krueger leaves the specifics to future researchers. "Like Newton," he concludes, "I hope I have offered the reader a few shiny pebbles; and while I hold some of those pebbles quite dear, it is very clear to me that cognitive science offers an ocean of great ideas, theories, and methods that entrepreneurship scholars and educators can explore for many years. There are smoother pebbles and prettier shells yet to be found."

Indeed, the lack of durable findings on the distinctive characteristics of business entrepreneurs has prompted a number of dead ends. "As intellectually stimulating as it may be to find out what motivates entrepreneurs and how they differ from ordinary mortals," Howard E. Aldrich and Martha Argelia Martinez wrote in 2001, "the more critical question is how these individuals manage to create and sustain successful organizations, despite severe obstacles." Writing later in the same article, they posed the central question for their field: "Can we really get to know the key features of those individuals who enter the heaven of successful entrepreneurship if we do not see the actions and circumstances of those who 'were not chosen'?"

Nevertheless, the search for the entrepreneurial type continues unabated and drives much of the contemporary study of social entrepreneurship. This search may be frustrating, but it is also critically important. Perhaps Echoing Green will find the answer through continued research and testing of its template for specifying the entrepreneurial qualities that lead to impact.

Conclusion

Words matter. By relying on lessons from business entrepreneurship and the concept of creative destruction, social entrepreneurship has become a powerful concept in the conversation about urgent threats. But business and social entrepreneurship are fundamentally different in many ways, most notably how the prevailing wisdom responds to new ideas.

Some argue, for example, that social entrepreneurship creates a new *and stable* equilibrium. But history strongly suggests that a new social equilibrium is almost inherently unstable. There have been great punctuations in modern history that have created lasting change—the New Deal and the Great Society produced lasting breakthroughs such as Social Security and Medicare, unemployment insurance and Head Start, and new regulatory regimes for the stock market and civil rights. But all of these breakthroughs are under fire today, and will continue to be far into the future. This is the nature of power and politics.

Ironically, some argue that the two great social movements of recent history have finally achieved their competing visions of the prevailing wisdom with passage of the 2010 health care reforms and the 2001 tax cuts. The former marks the supposed end of the New Deal, while the latter theoretically ends with the Reagan Revolution. Some pundits argue that these two versions of the prevailing wisdom are now completed into competing statutes and regulations, but neither is cemented. Both continue to battle each other in separate political movements, and are unlikely to be resolved soon.

Indeed, each of these visions is anchored in the very fabric of the U.S. Constitution and the ongoing political contests between political parties and interest groups. They are always at war to some extent, and anchor today's hyper-polarization on Capitol Hill and in the media. The two visions can find common ground during periods of war and domestic crisis, of course. But the visions compete constantly for victory on the major issues of the day, most notably on big-ticket reforms such as health care and economic recovery.

Thus, even as we celebrate the notable success of social entrepreneurship in creating new ideas for changing the prevailing wisdom about education, disease, hunger, and economic development, we must be cognizant of the pushback. Much as social entrepreneurs try to be nonpartisan, their ideas are often sliced and diced into political fodder by opponents.

Volunteerism is a great public good, for example, but paying for it is subject to debate as well-motivated citizens pick their issues and their favorite organizations, left or right. Even as we learn more about disciplined imagination, research and development, launch, market penetration, and scale-up from business, we must also learn from other disciplines as we develop techniques for diffusion and impact. Entrepreneurship not only has different purposes in the political and business worlds; it has very different tactics. Secrecy is the prime directive in business, for example, while transparency is a central value in government.

As such, social entrepreneurs must do more than create, launch, and scale new combinations of ideas. They have a longer-term job description, too:

- Design strategies for achieving lasting agitation.
- Create public support for breakthrough.
- Keep this support alive and focused on meaningful interventions.
- Lobby and campaign.
- Testify both literally and figuratively to the need for policy change.
- Support the faithful execution of the laws that social entrepreneurs' ideas produce.
- Build coalitions with safekeepers, explorers, and advocates to produce, maintain, update, and improve past breakthroughs.
- Insist on an adequate infrastructure for future breakthroughs.

- Celebrate the contributions of social networks even if this means less credit for the social entrepreneur's own organization.
- Prepare for counterattack.

Defined more broadly, the social entrepreneur's job description involves the steadfast application of creativity to both inventing new solutions and fighting for their adoption. They cannot assume that the world will follow their lead—they must recruit support wherever they can, even if this means a loss of distinctiveness.

As Jane Wei-Skillern and Sonia Marciano wrote in the spring 2008 *Stanford Social Innovation Review*, social breakthrough requires a new kind of social-benefit organization:

> Management wisdom says that nonprofits must be large and in charge to do the most good. But some of the world's most successful organizations instead stay small, sharing their load with like-minded, long-term partners. The success of these networked nonprofits suggests that organizations should focus less on growing themselves and more on cultivating their networks.

Unlike business breakthroughs, which must be concentrated in a single organization or supply chain to achieve profit, social breakthrough is strengthened by widespread collaboration with potential competitors.

Wei-Skillern and Marciano found few distinctly business-like characteristics among the members of successful networks. To the contrary, social impact came first, not proprietary interest and intellectual property. Members put their missions first even if they had to forsake benefits such as credit, control, funding, and growth. In doing so, they spread risk across many partners, thereby reducing their own vulnerability. By viewing themselves as nodes, not hubs, of their networks, they continued their own discreet work but benefited from "more holistic, coordinated, and realistic solutions to social issues" than traditional hub organizations.

Building these nodes of impact is now part of the social entrepreneur's job description, too.

Chapter 2

Agitating the Prevailing Wisdom

New combinations of ideas come in several forms—products, production systems, waste recovery, efficiency, and so forth. Some new combinations are entirely unexpected, while others involve easily recognizable innovation and expansion of well-known ideas.

Social entrepreneurship is clearly designed to produce new combinations. But new combinations also arise with constant vigilance of past breakthrough, on-the-fly innovation during implementation, early alertness regarding emerging threats, and aggressive attacks on the prevailing wisdom, which economists call the social equilibrium, political scientists call the distribution of power, and sociologists call social norms. But whatever it is called, the prevailing wisdom is highly resistant to change—that is how it remains the prevailing wisdom.

Changing the prevailing wisdom requires intense agitation toward a new prevailing wisdom by simultaneously signaling intended change and upsetting business as usual. At least for the purpose of broadening the inventory of options for agitation, let me suggest that social breakthrough involves at least four drivers: (1) social entrepreneurship, (2) social safekeeping, (3) social exploring, and (4) social advocacy.

Each driver has its own dynamics: Social entrepreneurship faces its greatest challenge in taking its ideas to scale, whether defined as growth or replication; social safekeeping faces its greatest challenge in finding the resources to innovate under unrelenting pressure to deliver goods and services; social exploring hits its most serious obstacles when it tells an inconvenient truth; and social advocacy is almost always under fire as too hot, too partisan, and too confrontational. Having discussed social entrepreneurship in the previous chapter, I provide in the following pages a deep examination of three other forms of agitation as complementary approaches.

As this book strongly suggests, these four drivers are just drivers. The decision to use one, two, or even all four drivers simultaneously must reflect the hoped-for effects. Instead of working forward through a simplistic logic chain of inputs (urgent threats), activities (imagining, inventing, and so forth), outputs (social entrepreneurship), and outcomes (breakthroughs), we might think about working backward from destination to driver—again, let the form of agitation follow the function. There will always be a role for social entrepreneurship, but we must also make room for other forms of social agitation as well. And all must accept the added burden of protecting the change they produce, a point made at the end of this chapter.

Social Safekeeping

Like any new endeavor, social entrepreneurship has worked hard to separate itself from other forms of social action. Although this distinctiveness is essential for generating enthusiasm and the funding that goes with it, it can also be a trap for false dichotomies between new and old ideas and between past breakthroughs and future endeavors both small and large. The emphasis on distinctiveness can also alienate potential partners and activate strong adversaries.

The more social entrepreneurship is defined by what it is *not*, meaning not social safekeeping or social advocacy, the less it can play its important role in the breakthrough cycle. Social entrepreneurship must avoid the distinctiveness trap that has isolated so many other fields in the past. With collaboration at the top of the agenda, social entrepreneurs need as many allies as they can find.

Roger Martin and Sally Osberg were aware of the challenge in writing their 2007 article: "Our goal is not to make an invidious comparison between the contributions made by traditional social service organizations and the results of social entrepreneurship, but simply to highlight what differentiates them."

But in further clarifying the distinctions several pages later, Martin and Osberg may have done just that (my emphasis added):

> The first type of social venture is social service provision. In this case, a courageous and committed individual identifies an unfortunate stable equilibrium—AIDS

> orphans in Africa, for example—and sets up a program to address it—for example, a school for the children to ensure that they are cared for and educated. The new school would certainly help the children it serves and may very well enable some of them to break free from poverty and transform their lives. But unless it is designed to achieve large scale or is so compelling as to *launch legions of imitators and replicators*, it is not likely to lead to a new superior equilibrium.
>
> These types of social-service ventures *never break out of their limited frame*: Their social breakthrough remains constrained, their service area *stays confined to a local population*, and their scope is determined by whatever resources they are able to attract. *These ventures are inherently vulnerable*, which may mean disruption or loss of service to the populations they serve. Millions of such organizations exist around the world—well-intended, noble in purpose, and frequently exemplary in execution—but they should not be confused with social entrepreneurship.

Much as one can appreciate Martin and Osberg's effort to draw sharp distinctions in search of definitional clarity, they understate the social entrepreneurship that already occurs in many social service agencies.

Social service providers are much more than rule-bound bureaucrats who never alter history. Their work not only is central to ameliorating the consequences of deprivation, but can play a central role in all aspects of social change. They are also primary safekeepers of past social breakthroughs.

The term *safekeeper* should be familiar to those who act as guardians and conservators for aging parents. Their job is not just to prevent physical and emotional harm. It is also to maintain their parents' health and strength for as long as possible, guarantee comfort and care, protect and build financial reserves, and bring together partners in innovative ways to enhance quality of life. They must maintain the social safety net, repair it when it fails, imagine new ways of enhancing quality of life, and maintain the care network. It is a blend of traditional defense, innovation, and anticipation—in short, proactive protection.

Social safekeeping involves a similar responsibility in defending and explaining past breakthroughs, repairing breakdowns, innovating toward better outcomes, measuring results, and expanding what already works. The defender's mission starts with protecting what we already have. Hunger would be even more threatening at home and abroad without food stamps and the Food for Peace Program, for example. Similarly, pandemics would be even more threatening without ongoing research at the National Institutes of Health, vaccination programs, and monitoring of new diseases such as H1N1 swine flu. And the 2010 health reform bill would not have passed without input from public health workers, hospitals, clinics, and other social safekeepers who used their muscle and community networks to deliver on a promise made more than a century ago.

The American Cancer Society was a particularly active participant in this advocacy. Although it is just the kind of large, old organization that is sometimes marginalized as too moribund to act, its mission contains all the elements of the safekeeper's job description: "The American Cancer Society is the nationwide, community-based, voluntary health organization dedicated to eliminating cancer as a major health problem by preventing cancer, saving lives, and diminishing suffering from cancer, through research, education, advocacy, and service."

Its 2008 decision to spend $14 million on an advocacy campaign for universal health care was a signal moment in its drive for social breakthrough. Even though its campaign was astutely nonpartisan, the organization knew that some of its largest corporate contributors might (and actually did) break away and a handful of board members might (and did) resist. However, the decision was true to the society's mission—cancer breakthroughs are of little value without access to treatment. Ironically, the American Cancer Society was drawn into the battle in part because cancer victims were reporting increased difficulty getting access to care on the toll-free telephone lines. It was social safekeeping that led to social impact, not vice versa. And its social exploring through seed grants to young researchers was central, too.

Safekeepers do more than defend the past; they also repair the damage from complacency and counterattacks, expand the reach of promising ideas, create new innovation, and remind society about the great potential for the future. Whereas business entrepreneurs disrupt the economic equilibrium permanently, social entrepreneurs cannot be sure their change will last. Eight-track tapes are gone forever, but not efforts to deregulate the banking industry, privatize Social Security, or stop stem cell research; typewriters may be gone for good, but not calls for nullification of federal laws. Again, the old social equilibrium never fades away—it merely waits for an opportunity to reassert itself. As such, the link between business and social entrepreneurship is often strained.

Consider the social safekeeper's job description:

- Defend past breakthroughs from erosion and budget cuts.
- Mend past breakthroughs that have eroded through disinvestment.
- Provide an authentic voice for expanding past breakthroughs.
- Pursue past endeavors that never reached fruition.
- Develop new measurement approaches for proving social breakthrough.
- Design, test, and implement innovations that produce greater social breakthrough.
- Test new ideas before scale-up using large test beds.
- Develop, adopt, and/or acquire new innovations.
- Develop, test, and launch innovations in what safekeepers deliver and how they deliver it.
- Scale-up new ideas using connections to other social safekeepers.
- Test and implement new organizational forms for improved productivity.
- Incubate new ideas, develop effective idea generators, and contribute to social exploring.
- Act as a fiscal agent for new ideas/organizations.
- Provide insights from day-to-day practice that can inform social entrepreneurship and fuel social advocacy.
- Translate lessons learned from practice into policy proposals.
- Partner with researchers to expand the knowledge base.
- Provide training opportunities for young and encore entrepreneurs.
- Generate collective support for programs that are already proven in ameliorating and addressing urgent threats; one example is the Earned Income Tax Credit, which has produced gains in reducing poverty.

A Caveat

Not all safekeepers embrace this broad job description. Nor do all do their jobs well. We can all name organizations and subsectors that have become highly bureaucratized barriers to the social breakthrough they once sought. We can also name individual safekeepers who seem more interested in their own survival (and compensation) than making a difference. And we can name safekeepers who are simply irrelevant in ongoing debates about the future. As one of my colleagues wrote to me regarding an earlier draft of this chapter, "We have to be careful that we're not falling into defending ancient history. We can't always be defending dinosaur institutions that are lumbering, inefficient, ineffective, and an anachronism in this rapidly changing world."

Moreover—and this may be the most important "moreover" in the book—some social safekeepers become so entrenched and defensive that they may become part of the prevailing wisdom that must be dismantled. Again, we all can think of social safekeepers who are part of the old equilibrium that fights to survive, whether because their own survival is at stake, their workforces have lost their purpose, or they reap enormous power from their continued dominance within a field.

Adding Value

Even as they deliver the goods and services created by past breakthroughs, social safekeepers also produce their share of innovation. Contrary to the conventional wisdom that social entrepreneurship is a 24/7 task, innovation often emerges from incubators, innovation funds, assorted idea generators such as suggestion programs and what some call *intrapreneurship*, and the more general collaborative creativity that can and often does occur within large organizations.

As if to confirm this hypothesis, an April 2010 report by the Johns Hopkins University Listening Post Project showed that 82 percent of the 417 nonprofits that participated in its latest assessment had implemented an innovative program or service within the past five years.

Acknowledging that more than half of the respondents came from Michigan, the survey showed innovative activity at small, medium, and large nonprofits. As the project's director, Lester Salamon, said, "Given the focus of both the Obama administration officials and U.S. foundation leaders on identifying and supporting innovative programs that truly work to address our nation's long-standing social challenges, it is highly encouraging to see that the innovative spirit appears to be alive and well in the core of the nation's nonprofit sector, and not just among new start-ups."

Indeed, social safekeepers may have special assets that make their innovations more likely to take hold, including research funding, dissemination outlets, and the authority that comes from day-to-day contact with the marginalized populations that social entrepreneurship seeks to help. Their organizations are often far from perfect, which suggests perhaps that they should focus more on how they work than on what they deliver. But it is a mistake to dismiss social safekeeping as just a tool of social service provision. Urgent threats can be addressed anywhere provided the resources exist.

The problem, of course, is finding those resources in an era of great scarcity. According to the Listening Post Project, nearly two-thirds of the nonprofits that responded to its survey said they had had at least one innovation in the past two years that could not be implemented. Of those respondents, 86 percent said they just did not have the funding, including a lack of growth capital, tight government funding streams, and the well-known foundation tendency to encourage innovation on a shoestring budget.

Social safekeepers also provide platforms for expansion. Geoffrey Canada's acclaimed Harlem Children's Zone is a perfect example. Although Canada is rightly credited for creating an innovative model for increasing student achievement, he acted as one part social entrepreneur and one part social safekeeper.

Indeed, the Harlem Children's Zone actually began its organizational journey in 1970 as the Rheedlen Centers for Children and Families. Despite its formal name change to the Harlem Children's Zone in the late 1990s, Rheedlen is easily reached through a simple Google search, and the organization is still identified by its original name by one of its major funders, the Annie E. Casey Foundation. The point here is not to confuse names, but to note the value in combining social entrepreneurship with social safekeeping.

Finally, social safekeepers create, preserve, and expand the social trust that Robert Putnam wrote about in *Bowling Alone*. As Putnam argued in 2000, there are two types of social capital: bonding capital and bridging capital. The two are not in conflict:

> In order to explain why, I need to remind you of an important distinction now commonly made in the field of social capital—that is, the distinction between "bonding" social capital (ties to people who are *like* you in some important way) and "bridging" social capital (ties to people who are *unlike* you in some important way). So, my bonding social capital consists of my ties to other white, male, elderly professors, and my bridging

> social capital reflects my ties to people of a different generation or a different race or a different gender. Too often, without really thinking about it, we assume that bridging social capital and bonding social capital are inversely correlated in a kind of zero-sum relationship: If I have lots of bonding ties, I must have few bridging ties, and vice versa. As an empirical matter, I believe that assumption is often false.

Social safekeepers create both kinds of social capital. They *bond* communities of like-minded individuals through their programs and *bridge* to other organizations and communities through their networks. As the stock of social capital increases, so does the possibility that communities will come together to produce social breakthrough. Although many social entrepreneurs such as Darell Hammond and his team at KaBOOM! often create social capital through strong community engagement (KaBOOM! builds a playground only after organizing a community), social safekeepers play a particularly significant role in both cultivating, banking, and spending social capital to protect, mend, maintain, and expand society's greatest achievements.

Social Exploring

Social exploring is the most important term to be added to the social breakthrough cycle discussed in the next chapter. It involves an explicit effort to evaluate past programs, interpret present threats, and monitor future trends and opportunities. These activities are essential for creating disruption and ultimate impact.

The ability to see into an uncertain future is particularly important for social breakthrough. And it requires much more than hunch, magic, or some kind of eerie mysticism. Explorers, like business entrepreneurs, appear to have a special set of skills that allow them to detect subtle changes in the social equilibrium that reveal an opportunity for impact.

Consider the social explorer's job description:

- Identify promising opportunities for disrupting the social equilibrium.
- Develop trend lines and signposts that signal urgent threats and tipping points.
- Extract lessons learned from the breakthrough cycle.
- Transfer promising innovations from the research community to the world of practice.
- Evaluate promising demonstration projects.
- Translate effective programs and practices into usable language for policy makers, investors, and other disseminators, scalers, and adopters.
- Research the social, economic, and political determinants of urgent threats.
- Develop inventories of potential surprises.
- Scan beyond the horizon for as-yet-unknown threats.
- Examine potential unknown unknowns (unk-unks) and surprises that might unsettle the social equilibrium and/or efforts to disrupt it.
- Develop partnerships that provide hard facts about the futures we face.
- Confront distortions in the deployment of facts by advocates and adversaries of social breakthrough.

Social explorers face two problems fulfilling their mission.

The first problem is that social exploring requires time, resources, and funding, all of which are in scarce supply in a time of urgent threats. Given a choice between a longitudinal study of a new idea or a quick scale-up, most investors jump at a scale-up. Rare is the investor who asks for more data. Hunch is often the driver—"We know it when we see it."

The second problem is that social explorers often produce uncomfortable results. Much as we all talk about logic chains, social rates of return on investment, data-driven decisions, outcome measurement, results management, and businesslike thinking, many consumers view explorers like me as rather like babies on an airplane—sometimes cuddly, often exhausting, occasionally irritating, and potentially dangerous.

Ironically, social explorers can be particularly irritating to social entrepreneurs, especially ones who are convinced that they are on the right course. Too many build their interventions off a single trend line that takes the past into the future, which political scientists often call "the science of muddling through." But once the social explorer speaks, social entrepreneurs, safekeepers, and advocates must accept the truth.

Tools for Exploring

Entrepreneurs and other actors can use a variety of exploratory means to assess the course of change—the more rigor they use, the more valuable their findings. Whatever the tool, the key is to think in "futures tense," meaning the constant search among the many possible futures we face. The following pages discuss five techniques for doing so: (1) the Delphi method, (2) exploratory analysis, (3) anticipating surprise, (4) assumption-based planning (ABP), and (5) robust decision making.

Many of these tools were developed and fine-tuned by the RAND Corporation. RAND is an international think tank once best-known for its work on nuclear deterrence. Created immediately after World War II, RAND has since expanded its exploring to a host of domestic issues such as education, health care, and even the arts. Once known as a comfortable home for neoconservatives, it is now quite accurately described as nonpartisan. It is astutely unwilling to accept the prevailing wisdom regardless of the political consequences.

Its five main exploratory methods are discussed next. All of the interviews came from the research leading to my book *The Four Pillars of High Performance.*

The Delphi Method. Named for the home of Greece's greatest oracle, the Delphi technique actually involves a highly rigorous system of anonymous interaction with a panel of outside experts who are asked to imagine alternative futures that can be used to encourage immediate action.

The Delphi method is anything but occult or oracular, however. As RAND's resident expert on the technique, James Dewar, explained the tool to me in 2003, the Delphi method is "used in strategic planning to project future technical, market, and other developments, uncover fundamental differences of opinion, and identify nonconventional ideas and concepts. Participants first make initial projections of future events. After their initial projections are correlated and shared with the group, participants are then asked to explain (anonymously) their differences in a series of follow-up rounds."

The questions used in a Delphi process can be a bit unusual, to say the least. Consider how Dewar once posed a question about energy policy in the year 2020:

> A time traveler from 20 years in the future will visit you early in the new millennium. The time traveler knows everything about the situation surrounding

energy needs in the year 2020. What do you want to know about the future?

Unusual though such questions might be, they produce plenty of outside-the-box thinking about future trends. After three rounds of back-and-forth, Dewar's expert panel of 27 academics, government officials, and industry leaders agreed that the most important questions about the future clustered around global warming, hybrid/zero-emission automobile markets, natural gas, increased nuclear power use, oil prices, and the viability of fuel cells.

Moreover, repeated experiments have shown that the Delphi technique does a much better job at projecting certain futures than high-powered, data-fueled mathematical models. If not informed by the Greek gods, experts appear to bring a mix of both judgment and data to bear on the questions they are asked.

Exploratory Analysis. Given the great uncertainty in today's world, no one involved in social change can take any future as a given. To the contrary, they must accept the reality that many futures are possible. At least for me, this is the most important lesson from my past work on social innovation and organizational performance. "Forecasting is inevitably a hazardous business," RAND's former director, Charles Wolf, wrote in 2008. "To paraphrase Yogi Berra, 'It's dangerous to make predictions, especially about the future.'"

Because RAND rejects the notion that any one future is knowable, it has specialized in developing methodologies for exploring inventories of possibilities. Although some futures may be more likely than others, RAND generally recommends that organizations take control of their destinies by thinking in futures tense, thereby abandoning the old predict-then-act model of action in favor of an explore-then-adapt approach that produces strategies that do well across a landscape of possibilities.

Many social entrepreneurs, safekeepers, explorers, and advocates already accept the notion that they face many futures, the only problem being that they only look at one or two futures at a time, often in isolation. The planning department may have one scenario of the future, the marketing department may have another, and the financial department may have still another. Instead of reasoning across a range of plausible futures, they often rush to define the most likely future.

The challenge is not to build consensus around a single future, however. It is to make sure that we understand the range of futures that might affect a breakthrough. For those who operate in stable environments, doing so might involve little more than an occasional conversation built around signposts, or harbingers, of possible change. Under conditions of light turbulence, organizations make fewer assumptions about the future and face less vulnerability as a result. But as turbulence rises, so do the number of assumptions about the future and the vulnerabilities to surprise.

The key term here is *possible futures*. Organizations are not required to imagine every alternative world out there. But they can develop very broad landscapes containing a wide range of possible, if not probable, futures. Just because there is no rain in the forecast does not mean rain is impossible. It is one of many possible futures that might require a bit of action such as carrying an umbrella. Some of these futures are just possible, but others are highly probable. The key to success involves creating landscapes first, then assigning rough probabilities for making decisions.

In an ideal world, we would all adopt the plan that performs best across a landscape of hundreds, if not thousands, of futures, and let events take their course. However, the world is anything but ideal, and the future anything but fixed. Almost by definition, we may end up adopting a less-than-ideal plan that performs reasonably well against all possible futures, but not necessarily best against the future that actually appears.

The answer is not to abandon the careful stewardship of scarce resources by building huge reserve funds, though a modest fund is essential, but to adapt as events unfold. However, we cannot adapt without some sense of potential threats and opportunities, which is why social explorers must create signposts, or checkpoints, well into the future. Signposts reveal an important change in the validity or vulnerability of a key assumption about the future.

Whatever they are called, signposts constitute an early-warning system that helps organizations respond to impending change. Developing this skill is expensive and has spawned a separate research discipline called *semiotics*. We cannot create answers to every possible surprise. But we can create indicators that reveal the breakdown of our basic assumptions. Doing so is essential for thinking in futures tense.

Anticipating Surprise. RAND is just as fascinated by surprise as any think tank, in part because surprises are so common. As one of RAND's most creative thinkers about thinking in futures tense, Paul Davis, says, surprises are not occasional annoyances in an otherwise predictable world, but, rather, a common occurrence in every field. Few predicted the Cuban missile crisis, the fall of the Shah of Iran, the disintegration of the Soviet Union, the terrorist attacks on September 11, or the stunning collapse of the Iraqi army in the first days of the second Gulf War.

"Why do so many predictions fail and surprises occur?" Davis asked me in 2003 as part of my research for *The Four Pillars of High Performance*. "The reasons include the constant competition of measures and countermeasures, the tendency to keep weaknesses out of mind only to have them attacked by the adversary, prosaic failures of design or execution, and a failure to appreciate the frictions of war."

RAND has long believed that the way to deal with uncertainty is to think of the world as a complex system in which small events can have major consequences. Who knows where a repair convoy might turn? Who knows which bunker holds the target and how many civilians might be nearby? As Davis cautions, "Uncertainty is not only ubiquitous and large, but also impossible to get rid of by merely working hard to do so."

The point is never to develop a single scenario against which to hedge or shape. Rather, it is to develop a set of scenarios that allow one to test current action against alternative possibilities through techniques such as assumption-based planning (ABP). According to Robert Lempert, RAND's top expert on uncertainty-based planning, some events are simply impossible to predict: "No matter how inclusive the information-gathering, how effective the analytic tools and techniques, how profound our insights, and how careful the resulting preparations, the future is certain to follow drivers and offer events we did not imagine. Surprise takes many forms, all of which tend to disrupt plans and planning systems."

Assumption-Based Planning. Assumptions shape every aspect of social breakthrough—they help define problems, causes, and solutions, as well as images of the future. Social Security actuaries use three different sets of assumptions to describe the future, for example: worst-case, best-guess, and best-case. During the bitter debates surrounding the 1983 Social Security funding crisis, the actuaries actually used five estimates: worst-worst-case, worst-case, best-guess, and best-case estimates, plus a best-best-case estimate based on the Reagan administration's own budget forecasts, which the budget director described as a "rosy scenario."

RAND rarely accepts assumptions about the present as a given and has invented a simple technique for questioning present-tense assumptions. Appropriately labeled assumption-based planning (ABP), the technique is about as simple as they get. First, ABP identifies the important, or load-bearing, assumptions underpinning your plan. Second, ABP explores the vulnerabilities in those assumptions. Third, ABP defines easily tracked signposts of the impending collapse of a load-bearing assumption. Fourth, ABP illuminates potential shaping actions that might reduce vulnerabilities. Fifth, ABP clearly outlines hedging actions that will reduce the social breakthrough of vulnerabilities if they occur.

Assumption-based planning is best done when decision makers can compare their vision of the future against alternative "worlds." "In our usage," James Dewar and his colleagues wrote in 2002 in their easily readable introduction to the method, "a *world* is a hypothetical future situation in which a vulnerable assumption has been violated for one (or more) of the plausible reasons." They continued, "Such a world is not complete in the sense that it describes how every aspect of today's world has evolved. It is intended only to add to the plausibility of evolving from today's world into one in which the vulnerable assumption has changed."

Assumption-based planning is so simple that any organization can do it without spending a cent on an external consultant. All it requires is a commitment to questioning the assumptions that underpin a current plan. As such, it is not a planning technique per se; rather, it is a questioning technique. As Robert Lempert explained, "Assumption-based planning is a very nice framework for finding vulnerabilities. It's very cheap, and it's simple. . . . You've got a plan and you look for vulnerabilities."

For the young nonprofit, assumption-based planning can create a needed reality check about its very purpose for being; for the older manufacturing firm, assumption-based planning can force hard choices about a rapidly changing world. If a plan has no violated assumptions, organizations can move forward with a relatively small number of signposts that reveal important changes in the world—for example, funding cutbacks by a state government or radical innovation such as charter schools in an existing market. If a plan has violated assumptions, organizations can decide whether they can shape and hedge themselves out of the problem. If so, they can take appropriate action; if not, they must change the plan.

Robust Decision Making. Although no one has invented a mathematical crystal ball for imagining the future, RAND has invented a wide range of techniques—some formal, some informal, but all rigorous—to create a "scenario space" that includes a number of possible futures against which organizations can hedge. It is a crystal ball of a kind.

Some of those futures involve what RAND characterizes as deep uncertainty. "Basically," said Lempert, "deep uncertainty is when you don't know the model, you don't have agreement on the probabilities, and you don't have agreement on the value functions. If you've got a lot of uncertainty, but you can characterize all the probabilities, you can use some variation of standard decision analysis. If you're running an electric grid or building an airplane, you can use that pretty easily."

RAND's work on deep uncertainty is designed to develop maps of possible futures against which to plan. "I think what we're trying to do is really systemize and better support the types of thinking that people intuitively do," Lempert said. "We want to help them do it much better."

Unlike assumption-based planning, which requires little more than a curious mind and a small slice of time, robust adaptive planning demands an extensive interaction between humans and computers in search of a plan that fails the most gracefully. The focus is on robustness, not optimization, meaning that the most profitable plan may not be the safest. A plan can be said to be robust in that it has considered a variety of alternative futures, threats, and possibilities, and has come out with the best results. According to Lempert, robust decision making allows decision makers to look for unknown vulnerabilities with the help of a computer.

> The claim is that people are very good at seeing patterns and intuiting hypotheses, breaking logjams as it were. If you have a room full of people and everybody picks something different, then what do you do? People are pretty good at saying, "Gee, how about if we approach the problem this way and do this? We could reach a compromise. This will get us what we want."
>
> They're also good at games or challenges. If I come up and say that no one can think of any plausible future that can break this scenario, people are really good at coming up with things. There's the wonderful deep literature book from the new Nobel laureate saying that

> cab drivers can basically tell you all the things that people do wrong. They can see patterns where they don't exist. They convince themselves that things are true that they want to be true, which are demonstrably not true; you can spend a little more time showing they're not true in those group things. It's all that sort of stuff.

Social Advocacy

Alongside their effort to distance social entrepreneurship from traditional social service provision, Martin and Osberg drew a somewhat more ambiguous line between social entrepreneurship and social advocacy. They most certainly had good reasons in drawing a line between the two activities, not the least of which was protecting the reputation of giants such as Martin Luther King Jr. But their dichotomy pushed social advocacy into a liminal state nonetheless.

> A second class of social venture is social activism. In this case, the motivator of the activity is the same—an unfortunate and stable equilibrium. And several aspects of the actor's characteristics are the same—inspiration, creativity, courage, and fortitude. What is different is the nature of the actor's action orientation. Instead of taking direct action, as the social entrepreneur would, the social activist attempts to create change through indirect action, by influencing others—governments, NGOs, consumers, workers, etc.—to take action. Social activists may or may not create ventures or organizations to advance the changes they seek. Successful activism can yield substantial improvements to existing systems and even result in a new equilibrium, but the

strategic nature of the action is distinct in its emphasis on influence rather than on direct action.

This, too, is a distinction that may weaken potential alliances. The terms *influence* and *direct action* are almost impossible to separate—influence is direct action, while direct action can and often does involve influence.

Many social entrepreneurs would certainly reject the distinction. They seek direct influence every day, whether as political appointees, candidates for elective office, witnesses, writers, investigators, data scrapers, or even talking heads. Many of their organizations have strong outreach engines, and they have also been known to press Congress and state legislatures for the occasional earmark. Their success is often measured by policy impact and what Ashoka describes as "the adoption of a fellow's idea in the public sphere." It is not always clear how such change could occur without some effort by social entrepreneurs to interact with policy makers.

Except in rare circumstances, social entrepreneurship cannot create breakthroughs without at least some level of advocacy. Nor can social entrepreneurs scale their programs to mega-impact without the help of both the safekeepers who protect old and new breakthroughs alike, and the advocates who help remove the barriers to social breakthrough. Influence and direct action are not mutually exclusive terms; in fact, they are variants of the same concept.

Thus, it hardly makes sense to build a grand new venture only to face legislative barriers such as limits on the number of charter schools, choke points in vaccine distribution, restrictions on the nursing profession's scope of practice, micromanagement of the grant-making process, and so forth. In an age of urgent threats, social entrepreneurs must either scale at light speed or join with social safekeepers and advocates to produce immediate effects.

Ultimately, these partnerships involve the astute use of power. Yet, power is almost entirely missing from the contemporary conversation about social entrepreneurship. The word never appeared in Martin and Osberg's 2007 article, for example, and is almost never used in the broader conversation about power-laden concepts such as creative destruction and social disruption.

Today's social entrepreneurs know power matters, however. Many leading social entrepreneurs were early Obama supporters, for example, while others worked on his campaign and transition teams, and still others took high-level appointments in his administration. Yet, the field as a whole remains reluctant to embrace power as a tool of impact. Power is too often dismissed as a threat to success, in part because it often involves partisanship.

The history of great breakthroughs suggests otherwise: Power is an essential resource for addressing urgent threats such as inequality, marginalization, racism, and corporate excess. Astute nonpartisanship and bipartisanship are absolutely and fully welcome in the push for social breakthrough, but partisanship must be welcome, too. After all, politics is a game for those who show up.

Bornstein and Davis clearly acknowledge the role of power in their recent book.

> Social entrepreneurship 3.0 is concerned with building platforms that enable more people at every age to think and behave like changemakers *and* to help them work together powerfully in teams and in teams of teams. It looks to forge stronger linkages across cultural and disciplinary boundaries, particularly with business and

government, and facilitate the rapid circulation and sharing of solutions at the global level.

Even if they rarely talk about it, social entrepreneurs know that power matters but also recognize that partisanship sometimes goes with it. As hard as they work to find common ground across the battleground, they use whatever tactics are needed to succeed.

A Shared Job Description

Many change agents focus on creating a breakthrough as the final destination of their work, but their work is not over once a breakthrough occurs. Past breakthroughs need special care and protection, too, if only because they are so painfully easy to reverse. Thus, part of change is protecting past achievements even as they search for new opportunities for change.

Consider the past 60 years of U.S. economic, political, and social breakthrough as an example of the constant threats to social change more generally. Although the following pages focus entirely on the federal government's broad inventory of priorities for addressing urgent threats, it is important to note that social entrepreneurship often produces results without legislation at all. Although legislation and regulations sometimes codify their achievements, social entrepreneurs often create breakthroughs by changing norms and attitudes, free trade being a powerful example.

Even the great social movements of the past have often relied on legislation and regulations to advance, punctuate, and cap their breakthroughs. The U.S. civil rights movement produced two great pieces of legislation and the 24th amendment to the U.S. Constitution; the education reform movement has produced a cascade of waivers and basic changes in federal and state legislation; the hospice movement has moved forward with new sources of public funding; and large-scale changes in governance often result in new legislation and regulation covering everything from ethics to transparency.

Nevertheless, the fact that so many of the federal government's great breakthroughs of the past 60 years are now imperiled is a warning sign regarding a part of the change agent's work that is yet to be broadly defined. It is not enough to secure a breakthrough. Breakthroughs must be protected from complacency and attack.

There is no doubt that change makers made great progress in forging an audacious inventory of government achievement between World War II and the new millennium. Name a significant domestic or foreign problem since 1945 and the federal government made some effort to solve it, sometimes through massive new programs such as Medicare and Apollo, other times through a string of smaller initiatives to address enduring problems such as disease and poverty. Looking back from the early years of our new millennium, it is difficult not to be proud of what the United States has tried to achieve over the past 60 years.

The proof is in the U.S. statute books. All told, Congress passed more than 500 major laws between 1945 and 2000 to improve the quality of life in the nation (and world). Having emerged victorious from the Great Depression and World War II, Congress called upon the federal government to tackle a bold agenda worthy of greatness, and provided the statutory authority to act. Convinced that the nation could achieve great dreams, Congress asked its citizens to do just that.

From Agitation to Breakthrough

As I argued in my 2002 book *Government's Greatest Achievements*, the nation did more than aim high. Working through government, business, and nonprofits, the United States produced a long list of breakthroughs. Much as Americans believe that the federal government creates more problems than it solves, my research suggests that government deserves more credit than it receives for all four drivers of social change.

Based on interviews with 450 of the nation's leading historians and political scientists in the summer of 1999, I scored government's greatest breakthroughs since World War II by putting the heaviest weight on success, while awarding extra credit for tackling especially important and difficult problems. This approach produces the following top-10 list of the greatest U.S. breakthroughs between World War II and the dawn of the new millennium. Note the enormous impact of legislative action for social change.

1. *Rebuild Europe after World War II.* Rebuilding Europe is the oldest endeavor on the top-10 list, and is anchored in the Foreign Assistance Act of 1948, better known as the Marshall Plan. It is also the only endeavor on the top-10 list that is no longer active. Launched with the Bretton Woods Agreement of 1945, the nation could declare success by the end of the 1950s.
2. *Expand the right to vote.* Ten statutes comprise this broad effort to protect and expand the right to vote. Although the Voting Rights Act of 1965 is the flagship on the list, it shares the endeavor with three extensions in 1970, 1975, and 1982; three earlier statutes (in 1957, 1960, and the Civil Rights Act of 1964); and two constitutional amendments

(the 24th outlawing the poll tax and the 26th lowering the voting age to 18), making it an endeavor of notable endurance.

3. *Guarantee equal access to public accommodations.* This three-statute endeavor originates in the Civil Rights Act of 1964, expands with the Open Housing Act of 1968, and is capped with the Americans with Disabilities Act of 1990. As such, it shares one of its three statutory foundations with the effort to eliminate workplace discrimination and expand the right to vote, confirming the enormous social breakthrough of the Civil Rights Act as an essential driver of impact both then and now and as arguably the single most important statute of the post–World War II period.
4. *Reduce disease.* The Polio Vaccination Act of 1955 is the starting point for a long list of interventions that have increased the human life span. Alongside vaccination assistance, the effort to reduce disease also includes targeted research on heart disease, cancer, and stroke; bans on smoking; strengthening the National Institutes of Health; and lead-based poison prevention. Despite this dispersion, the endeavor reflects a clear commitment to reducing disease, whether through specific interventions or through broad research investments.
5. *Reduce workplace discrimination.* Seven statutes anchor this effort to prohibit workplace discrimination based on race, color, religion, gender, national origin, age, or disability. This breakthrough received its greatest boosts under the Civil Rights Act of 1964, the Age Discrimination Act of 1967, and the Americans with Disabilities Act of 1990. It is a classic example of how an initial breakthrough statute

such as the Civil Rights Act can provide a wedge for further expansion over time.

6. *Assure safer food and drinking water.* Nine statutes comprise this long-running bipartisan effort, including the Federal Insecticide, Fungicide, and Rodenticide Act of 1947 (signed by Harry Truman), Poultry Products Inspection Act of 1957 (signed by Dwight Eisenhower), Wholesome Meat and Poultry Acts of 1967 and 1968 (signed by Lyndon Johnson), Federal Environmental Pesticide Control Act (signed by Richard Nixon), the Safe Drinking Water Act of 1974 (signed by Gerald Ford), and the Food Quality Protection Act of 1996 (signed by Bill Clinton).
7. *Build a national highway system.* Eight statutes underpin the ongoing federal effort to augment the national highway system, most notably the 1956 Interstate Highway Act. The multibillion-dollar expansions of highway aid under the 1991 Intermodal Surface Transportation Act and 1998 Transportation Equity Act for the Twenty-First Century make this endeavor the most recently amended on the list, except for health care reforms.
8. *Expand health insurance for older Americans.* Medicare is the flagship of this highly concentrated, three-statute endeavor, which also includes the relatively small-scale Kerr-Mills 1960 precursor to Medicare and the now-defunct Medicare Catastrophic Coverage Act of 1988. As such, this is the only endeavor on the top-10 list that involved a single breakthrough statute that defined the breakthrough, and later provided the momentum for the Children's Health Insurance Program and the 2010 health care reforms.
9. *Reduce the federal budget deficit.* Six statutes fall under the effort to balance the federal budget through caps, cuts,

and tax increases, including the Gramm-Rudman-Hollings Anti-Deficit Act of 1985, and the 1987, 1990, 1993, and 1997 deficit reduction/tax increase packages that contributed to the budget surpluses, which were squandered in the early 2000s.

10. *Expand financial security for older Americans.* Twenty-one statutes comprise the effort to reduce poverty among the elderly through expanded benefits, pension protection, and individual savings, including 12 increases in Social Security benefits and two broad rescue attempts, the 1972 amendments to the Social Security Act that created the Supplemental Security Income program, and the Employment Retirement Income Security Act.

Three Simple Lessons from the Past. There are three simple lessons from these "greatest hits." First, breakthrough requires significant collaboration across the aisles and institutions. Neither Democrats nor Republicans can be credited with any specific breakthroughs. Although one party might have driven the initial breakthrough, both parties eventually embraced the idea. Even Medicare, which was a signature accomplishment of Lyndon Johnson's Great Society, and the Marshall Plan, which carried Harry S. Truman's imprimatur, had antecedents in earlier congresses and administrations.

Second, breakthrough involves persistence and a mix of incremental adjustment punctuated by occasional grand decisions. Although there are great statutes on the list, the United States achieved most of its successes by wearing down the prevailing wisdom, often through incremental adjustments in early gains. The nation did not reduce disease with a single act, for example, but with dozens of statutes over the years; nor did it achieve scientific and technological breakthroughs with one research and development grant. But who were the agitators? If the preservation of social breakthrough is as important as the agitation, what is the history of the agitators who wore down the prevailing wisdom to break through? Martin Luther King Jr. assembled a network of agitators, which led to greatest hit number two, for example.

Finally, breakthrough resides in an abiding commitment to the cause, whether a belief in human equality, a commitment to world peace and democracy, or a commitment to honoring promises to previous generations. No one knew at the time whether expanding the right to vote, opening public accommodations, or ending workplace discrimination would eventually succeed. Nor did anyone have a defensible cost-benefit analysis to prove that the United States would succeed. Yet, the nation endeavored nonetheless, often taking the moral high ground despite significant resistance.

Breakthroughs in Peril

Just as one can look back with considerable awe at what the federal government tried to accomplish over the past half-century, so, too, can one look forward with considerable doubt about whether government will ever be so bold again.

For the moment, however, the most urgent threat we face may be the erosion of our past breakthroughs. Of the top 30 breakthroughs that made my 2002 list, all but one, the Marshall Plan, is under siege. And I could easily argue that the current financial meltdowns in Greece, Portugal, Spain, and Turkey raise questions about the durable effect of even that once-great breakthrough. The breakthroughs and their current statuses are summarized in Table 2.1. As the list suggests, there are at least 29 urgent threats on the horizon simply because of the benign and deliberate neglect of past breakthroughs.

Table 2.1 Breakthroughs in Peril

Rank	Breakthrough	Imperiled?	Reason
1	Rebuild Europe after World War II.	No	Completed.
2	Expand the right to vote.	Yes	Voting rights are breaking down with failed technologies and partisan redistricting.
3	Guarantee equal access to public accommodations.	Yes	Access to public accommodations is now challenged by redlining and concentrated disinvestment in public space.
4	Reduce disease.	Yes	Reducing disease is hobbled by antiquated laboratories and underfunding.
5	Reduce workplace discrimination.	Yes	Workplace discrimination is rising with economic stress and pink slips.
6	Assure safer food and drinking water.	Yes	Safe food and drinking water are threatened by administrative negligence, intense lobbying, and the rise of an entirely new generation of chemical and biological toxins.
7	Build a national highway system.	Yes	The nation's highway system is rusting away with cuts in infrastructure funding.
8	Expand health insurance for older Americans.	Yes	Health security for older Americans is under siege by the extraordinary yearly increase in costs.
9	Reduce the federal budget deficit.	Yes	The budget surplus is gone, and the national debt is rising fast.
10	Expand financial security for older Americans.	Yes	Financial security for older Americans is reaching a breaking point with the onslaught of baby boom retirements.

Rank	Breakthrough	Imperiled?	Reason
11	Improve water quality.	Yes	Water quality is threatened as governments struggle to rebuild and expand antiquated technology.
12	Help veterans of war adjust to civilian life.	Yes	Help for veterans is at risk because of aging infrastructure, increased costs, and the new terrors of war.
13	Promote scientific and technological research.	Yes	The nation's scientific and technological engines are weakening with underinvestment in education.
14	Win the Cold War.	Yes	The Cold War may be over, but Russia remains a one-party state with hegemonic intentions.
15	Improve air quality.	Yes	Air quality is drifting away as carbon emissions continue to rise.
16	Guarantee workplace safety.	Yes	Workplace safety has been battered by the unwillingness to faithfully execute the laws.
17	Maintain the national defense.	Yes	The nation's military is stretched to the breaking point by the wars in Iraq and Afghanistan, equipment breakdowns, and procurement scandals.
18	Reduce hunger and improve nutrition.	Yes	Hunger is up, and access to nutritious food has become a battleground as government looks for discretionary budget cuts.
19	Increase access to postsecondary education.	Yes	College students face huge tuition increases and mounting debt.
20	Enhance consumer protection.	Yes	Faithful execution of the laws has been uneven.
21	Expand foreign markets for U.S. goods.	Yes	The U.S. trade deficit is rising at historic rates as foreign nations block U.S. exports.

(*Continued*)

Table 2.1 (*Continued*)

Rank	Breakthrough	Imperiled?	Reason
22	Increase financial and market stability.	Yes	Financial and market stability are distant memories as regulatory agencies collapse.
23	Control nuclear arms and encourage disarmament.	Yes	Nuclear proliferation remains a constant threat as rogue nations develop their capacity to produce weapons of mass destruction.
24	Protect the wilderness.	Yes	Past progress to protect the wilderness is on the cutting agenda.
25	Promote space exploration.	Yes	Even unmanned exploration is at risk in the current budget climate.
26	Protect endangered species.	Yes	Past progress is at risk with administrative roadblocks, budget cuts, and global warming.
27	Reduce exposure to hazardous waste.	Yes	The global economy has proven particularly creative at inventing new types of hazardous waste; the Superfund program is underfunded and sluggish; and past government regulations lag well behind the scientific evidence on the levels of harm.
28	Enhance the nation's health care infrastructure.	Yes	The nation's health care institutions are among the most expensive but are rusting and in disrepair.
29	Maintain stability in the Persian Gulf region.	Yes	There seems to be no resolution to the Middle East conflict and no such thing as stability in the Persian Gulf.
30	Expand home ownership.	Yes	Past gains in home ownership have been swept away by the foreclosure crisis.

Social entrepreneurs clearly have a significant role to play in reversing this damage, whether through new ideas for deeper impact, better methods to deliver effective services, or entirely new models for achieving similar goals. However, social safekeepers, explorers, and advocates must also engage. All four must challenge the prevailing wisdom that what's past is past.

Conclusion

The ongoing battle to create a distinctive vision of social entrepreneurship creates considerable confusion on the front lines of change, especially when success depends on a blend of drivers. If form follows function, path follows purpose, and means follow ends, then each of the four drivers of change has an important role in achieving different forms of agitation.

- If the agitation involves a new combination of ideas for change, then social entrepreneurship is likely to be the preferred driver.
- If the agitation involves the protection, repair, maintenance, fine-tuning, expansion, and further innovation of past breakthroughs, then social safekeeping is likely to be at the forefront.
- If the agitation involves an effort to anticipate key threats, monitor trends, and evaluate what does and does not work, then social exploring is likely to be the means to the end.
- If the agitation involves an effort to produce policy impact through lobbying, political pressure, and even partisanship, then social advocacy must be engaged.

Some readers might rightly ask which form of agitation comes first. At first glance, social exploring seems like a logical starting point in the breakthrough cycle. After all, explorers often identify the opportunities and targets for change, and are key participants in research and development.

Social entrepreneurship seems like a logical second step in agitating for change. After all, social entrepreneurs assemble the new combinations that help create a breakthrough.

Social advocacy seems like a logical third step as it exploits the pressure points for change. After all, even legions of replicators and imitators may not be able to create the pressure needed to create durable change.

Finally, social safekeeping seems like a logical resting place. After all, safekeepers implement, fine-tune, and convert the abstract outlines of a new prevailing wisdom into day-to-day practice.

Much as one might long for such order, the change process is rarely so logical. New ideas come from safekeepers, too, for example, while advocates often identify opportunities and targets for change. Explorers are usually engaged in all forms of agitation, especially in spotting trends that might reveal an urgent threat. And social entrepreneurs often engage in all four forms of agitation.

Consequently, it is risky to embrace strict views of what comes first. Although the next chapter provides some order in describing the breakthrough cycle, experience suggests that the journey to lasting change is fraught with backtracks, surprise, mystery, and wonder. Even as we try to map it more carefully by drawing on lessons from success and failure, the cycle is inherently messy, as is social change in general.

However, I do believe that breakthrough is more likely to occur when drivers are matched more closely to the destination at hand. I also believe that breakthrough is more likely to occur when all four drivers work together through breakthrough networks. As the next chapter shows, these networks are aggregators of impact—in theory, they merge the very best products of entrepreneurs, safekeepers, explorers, and advocates into a coherent, focused whole. By blurring the definitional boundaries that I believe have weakened the broad field of social change, we just might be able to meet the urgent threats before they overwhelm us.

Chapter 3

The Breakthrough Cycle

There is little disagreement that social entrepreneurship is a significant driver for changing the prevailing wisdom. There is also no doubt that there are other equally important drivers. New combinations of ideas are neither necessary nor sufficient for social change. Nor are efforts to expand and protect past breakthroughs, monitor the leading indicators of crisis, or create political pressure. All can lead to a new prevailing wisdom.

The challenge, therefore, is to put the instruments of agitation in their proper place in the overall breakthrough cycle. This cycle is in constant motion, sometimes moving forward in the wake of a crisis, election, or other opportunity for change, sometimes stalling as the prevailing wisdom fights back, and sometimes lurching backward as proposals for a more just world are rebuffed by the industries of deprivation that profit from the world's distress.

This chapter sorts these stages by describing the social breakthrough cycle and redefining the logic of change as it moves from initial commitment to a breakthrough proposal, agitation, aggregation, disruption, and enactment. The chapter moves forward with a discussion of possible targets for future research and exploration and ends with an introduction to the concept of *robust breakthrough networks*, meaning networks that have the agility, alertness, adaptability, and alignment to have maximum impact.

Driving Change

In the jargon of logic chains, social entrepreneurship is one of several forms of agitation in a social breakthrough cycle that moves from inputs, activities, and outputs to a new social equilibrium.

It is important to note that cycles are inherently mechanistic in tone. They assume that one must pass through each gate en route to the next. The breakthrough cycle should be viewed as much more pliable. Some organizations jump far ahead, turn around and revisit old issues, and move through a kind of liminal space as they pursue change.

At first glance, the breakthrough cycle looks like a stage-gate model in which change moves ever forward as gates close behind it. However, the breakthrough cycle is both unpredictable and messy. Writing with his colleague Douglas Polley in 1996, Van de Venn described the journey through the "rugged landscape" of innovation:

> We want to cross the dark valley to reach the peak on the other side. A broad goal galvanizes us to action. To reach the other side we must explore the valley at the same

> time we are constructing a path to the other side. We utilize our collective and individual skills by dividing up and sending scouts to pick specific paths from among the visible details of the valley (game paths, open versus thickly wooded areas, caves and canyons, etc.). Some are detoured in the maze of a cave, some get chased up a tree by wild beasts, others become preoccupied with cataloguing the vegetation along the trails, while others discover that the peak on the other side consists of a mountain range with many peaks. As we move forward and exert efforts in clearing our paths, we discover more about the terrain as well as ourselves. We become good at trail blazing, at learning what we like and dislike, but not necessarily at knowing where we will end up.

This journey can involve simple, linear steps from one stage to another, but can also involve dead ends, wandering, and great risk. Social change is never simple, and is certainly not easy. It is a journey best taken with purpose and perseverance.

Nevertheless, the breakthrough cycle is helpful for posing key questions that tend to flow naturally from one stage to the next. As Figure 3.1 shows, the social breakthrough cycle starts with the basic assets for impact and ends with a more just, tolerant, and equitable world, even if that world only covers 90 city blocks. Although each stage is linked by a one-way arrow, each one blends into the other and allows movement back and forth. The cycle is anything but orderly.

Stage 1: Are You Ready and Willing?

The first stage in social change involves a personal and/or collective commitment to social change. This commitment must be present throughout the cycle, and is the basis for creating

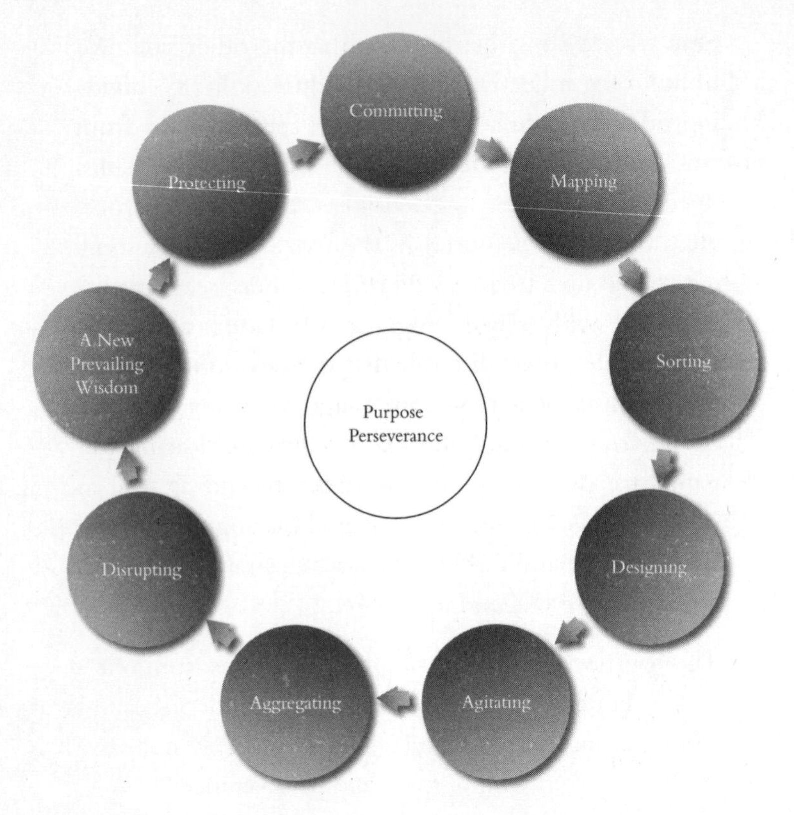

Figure 3.1 The Social Breakthrough Cycle

and sustaining change in every setting, be it government, nonprofit, or corporate. It is embedded in both purpose (the personal drive to create change) and perseverance (the willingness to engage for as long as it takes). Although commitment comes first in the cycle, it is ever present in the drive for change.

Stage 2: What Are Your Assets and Obstacles?

The second stage of the cycle involves a careful mapping of the assets and obstacles that shape ultimate success. There are *at least* five assets that temper or encourage social breakthrough in its first moments: (1) the demand for impact, (2) willingness to engage, (3) basic freedoms for impact, (4) institutional responsiveness, and (5) the faithful execution of impact.

It is hard to imagine a successful change effort without basic social, economic, and political freedom, for example. Citizens must express at least some demand for change—whether measured by their overall sense of economic stress, oppression, personal deprivation, lack of access to health care, environmental degradation, perceived government corruption, or any other measure. They must also express some willingness to engage, whether through their votes, petitioning, protests, or organizing. They must also have the basic freedoms needed for information and action such as freedom of the press, assembly, and other forms of direct action. And they must have a government that is both responsive and faithful in executing change.

These assets are often in short supply around the world, and frequently become the first targets for change. Sometimes citizen demand and political efficacy must be created, practiced, and most certainly aggregated. Other times, basic freedoms must be established and codified. Still other times, institutional responsiveness and faithful execution must be the target for change, especially when both are undermined by corruption and incompetence.

Stage 3: What Are the Options for Breaking Through?

The third stage of the cycle involves a deliberate and disciplined sorting process. It is designed to assemble the components of a breakthrough proposal, including everything from ideas (new and old) to opportunities, partners, organizations, platforms for influence, and even adversaries.

This sorting guides the early journey through what Paul Bloom and J. Gregory Dees call the "ecosystem" of change. This ecosystem contains everything from support (funding, demand, organizational capacity) to opposition, each one flowing through the system independently. The change agent's role is to pull from each stream in search of components for a high-impact new combination.

Like sorting the pieces of a jigsaw puzzle, this process produces the initial sketch of a breakthrough proposal. Sometimes careful sorting will produce an entirely new idea; other times, it will produce new methods for combining or activating an old idea. The goal is to create an inventory of options for moving through the design process described in the following pages. Done well, the process will produce the best idea for impact, be it new or old.

Oftentimes, the best combinations are found by simple trial and error. This is certainly the case in government. As Martin A. Levin and Mary Bryna Sanger wrote in 1994, most government innovation is anything but surprising:

> We found that public-sector innovations generally did not spring anew as if from blueprints, but evolved through an adaptive process. Their novelty more often was in their assemblage—often of familiar parts. Like natural selection, the evolutionary tinkering that ultimately produces innovation is messy. Organisms change and adapt; their ultimate fate is tested in the field. Evolutionary tinkering—using bits and pieces of what is around in new ways to meet changing circumstances—is iterative, incremental, and disorderly. Failure-and-error becomes the basis for evolutionary learning. Analysis occurs at the implementation stage, after a process that is begun to "do the doable."

Having examined 28 winners of the Ford Foundation's prestigious Innovation in Government Award, Levin and Sanger also concluded that the innovation is often "old stuff." The innovation comes from the new combination of familiar elements. "Managers innovate through a process of wandering around, informally listening and looking," they noted. "They pick up old stuff through an adaptive, trial-and-error process of aim-fire-ready. New plans change and adapt in response to assessments of actual field performance. We argue that this is both how successful practitioners in fact behave to develop innovative initiatives and how they ought to behave. They ought to because it is more effective and more realistic." Robert Behn famously described this process in 1988 as "management by groping along."

Stage 4: What Will You Propose and Where Will You Work?

The fourth stage uses these components to design a formal breakthrough proposal, whether contained in draft legislation, a demonstration project, an advocacy campaign, or the seeds of a social movement. This stage involves a range of tasks that are described in the literature on entrepreneurship: imagining, inventing, identifying opportunities, testing, launching, accelerating, scaling up, disseminating, and so forth.

The stage also involves a basic decision on where the breakthrough will be housed. Does it require an entirely new organization, with what that means for start-up costs and delay? Or can a breakthrough emerge from an existing organization, with what that means for bureaucratic delay and interference? The answer depends on the destination for change—form must follow function.

All too often, however, this creative process stalls at the scaling point, which involves moving a particularly powerful idea to higher visibility and impact, not just creating a bigger organization. Although the business equilibrium responds to the power of a good idea, scaling is much more uncertain in social breakthrough.

As with the cycle as a whole, this design phase is iterative in nature. The breakthrough idea is rarely formed in the first pass—it is imagined, shaped, tested, and developed into a workable, albeit often audacious, new combination. It can become an "idea in good currency" only if it can withstand the intense scrutiny it will encounter as it moves through the proof-of-concept stage. This willingness to question (and measure) is essential as ideas begin the effort to penetrate the existing equilibrium—so is the alertness to opportunities for action.

Stage 5: How Will You Take the Offense?

The fifth stage of the cycle involves a deliberate effort to agitate the prevailing wisdom through one of the four drivers of change: (1) social entrepreneurship (the new combinations that create waves of creative destruction); (2) social safekeeping (the protection, mending, maintenance, and expansion of past successes); (3) social exploring (the systematic, rigorous search for alternative futures that might produce opportunities for social breakthrough); and (4) social advocacy (the pursuit of durable impact on public policies).

These four drivers need not reside in different organizations. At the same time, there is increasing pressure on organizations to engage in partnerships to achieve greater impact. Agitation involves a series of discrete tasks that start with launching an idea for creating or defending change, accelerating to scale, and building further momentum toward breakthrough.

In essence, the four drivers of change work, separately or together, to create the irritation needed for disruption. Explorers are essential for identifying opportunities and highlighting trends; entrepreneurs and safekeepers engage in creating, proving, and launching the new combinations; and advocates take the new combinations forward.

Stage 6: How Will You Maximize Pressure?

The sixth stage of the cycle aggregates this agitation through economic, social, and/or political networks. These networks are composed of a dense collection of actors that includes entrepreneurs (and their organizations), safekeepers, explorers, and advocates who work together in a virtual space that concentrates their firepower for maximum effect.

Members of these networks usually involve a mix of entrepreneurs, safekeepers, explorers, and advocates. Working in concert through what the Skoll Foundation calls "catalytic collaboration," they join forces to create a wave of creative destruction that focuses on a specific opportunity for destabilizing the existing social equilibrium.

It is useful to note, however, that social breakthrough can occur without a breakthrough network. Although I believe breakthrough networks are the most powerful form of aggregation, there are examples of single new ideas that are sufficiently large and compelling to disrupt and replace the prevailing wisdom on their own—for example, the hospice and vaccination programs.

Some ideas are so powerful and entrepreneurs/innovators so fully equipped for aggregation that they exist as networks on their own. Despite the welcome revisionism about the definition of going to scale, there will always be organizations that are so big and well-resourced that they can create disruption without help. Even here, however, there are almost always networks that develop around them. In this sense, these organizations act as nodes of impact as others join their cause.

Stage 7: What Tactics Will You Use to Disturb the Prevailing Wisdom?

The seventh stage of the cycle involves an intense and focused effort to disrupt and displace the prevailing wisdom. The intention to disrupt is one thing, but actual impact is quite another. Using a variety of tactics that include hundreds of discrete activities that are shaped into a kind of explosive charge, breakthrough networks are designed to change the prevailing wisdom.

Using these tactics, the four drivers of social change pulse toward impact through swarming and other tactics. Their goal is simple: exploit every opportunity possible—policy (e.g., regulation, legislation, executive actions, etc.) and harness every resource to act (e.g., public opinion, social norms, expectations for future action).

These networks are often coordinated by a team of some kind, which is often built around a single breakthrough organization, its funders and sponsors, and a number of strategists, some of whom operate through contracts and subcontracts. Using the effects-based planning discussed later in this chapter, this team creates the robustness needed to produce sustained impact.

Stage 8: How Will You Secure Success?

The eighth stage of the cycle involves a sustained effort to secure the actual breakthrough via enactment, broadly defined. Although enactment is often used to describe a formal policy change such as legislation, the term has much broader meaning as a way to describe the realization of actual success through a variety of means. Policy is only a means to an end, just as changes in social norms and expectations for a more just world are.

Stage 9: How Will You Protect the New Wisdom?

The breakthrough cycle does not end with the actual enactment of the breakthrough. It continues with an almost inevitable and long-term effort to protect the breakthrough as it takes its place in a new prevailing wisdom.

Exploring the Cycle

Like the plan-do-check-act cycles that have reshaped modern industry, the social breakthrough cycle should be seen as continuous, especially since the old social equilibrium never quite disappears as its advocates fight to reclaim control of the prevailing wisdom. This is the point at which celebration, sharing credit, and maintenance become particularly important. It is also the point at which opportunities for expansion arise, whether from neighborhood to neighborhood, city to city, state to state, nation to nation, or across the globe, which is what triggers the new and stable equilibrium for the global society as a whole.

Admittedly, each stage of the social breakthrough cycle is highly complex. Each stage involves its own dynamics, tactics, process, and lessons learned. Researchers can and do spend entire careers trying to understand how to create the assets for impact, the sources of commitment to change, the methods for sorting the components of new combinations, approaches to designing new combinations, and so forth through the cycle.

As a first example, consider the interior of the creative stage. Having started with a burst of energy, inspiration, and creativity, this stage moves forward with the design of a specific idea, research and development, further testing, and the construction of an effective platform (form following function) for pushing forward, usually in the form of an elementary organization.

As a second example, consider the interior of the agitation stage. There is good research already in hand on scaling, for example, much of it built around the notion that scale does not mean size. As J. Gregory Dees argued in an April 6, 2010, posting on McKinsey & Company's What Matters Web site, the question is not *whether* social entrepreneurs can scale their ideas, but *how* they can do it:

> In reframing this as a "how can" question, I think we can be a bit more precise. With social entrepreneurs attacking time-sensitive social problems, we would like to increase the speed with which they can scale their impact. Given that many of them rely to some degree on relatively scarce resources, such as philanthropic dollars, it is important that they scale impact with an eye to the efficient use of those resources. Thus, we would be better served by focusing our intelligence and creativity on the question, "How can more social entrepreneurs achieve greater, that is, more widespread and lasting, impact sooner and more cost effectively?"

His answer is simple: "In thinking about the best ways to achieve large-scale change, we need to keep in mind that there are many different paths, and some of the most effective paths do not require growing an organization to large scale." Scale can involve everything from safekeeping to exploration and advocacy, including legislation and regulation. Government is not always the enemy; to the contrary, it contains many partners for action.

Scale also involves many paths, a point also well made by Dees in his posting:

> If we care about large-scale change, we need to keep in mind that social entrepreneurs can scale their impact by getting new legislation or regulations passed; getting old legislation or regulations enforced; shifting social norms, behaviors, and attitudes among fellow citizens, corporations, government personnel; changing the way markets operate; and finding ways to prevent the problems they have been solving or reducing the needs they have been serving. None of these methods of scaling impact necessarily requires massive organizational growth, which can slow the process down. The impact happens because of the activities of others. Thus, when we ask about scaling impact, we should also ask: "How can social entrepreneurs magnify and accelerate the scale of their impact by looking beyond simply growing their organizations or replicating their service models?"

As if to complicate the discussion, we also have to explore the links between each stage of the overall social breakthrough cycle—we might even put a bull's-eye on each arrow between the nine stages of the cycle, asking what moves the commitment to collection to creation to agitation and so forth. And we always need to remember that social breakthrough occurs in the ecosystem outlined by Bloom and Dees.

Luckily, there is considerable research about how to move from each stage of the overall cycle to breakthrough. For now, however, case studies and small samples are the markers of our progress on the targeting process. There is much more work to be done exploring each stage of the cycle and its links to eventual success. Given the work already done by scholars named earlier, I believe there are five particularly attractive targets for deeper social exploring: (1) committing to change, (2) mapping assets and obstacles, (3) designing an organizational home, (4) aggregating pressure, and (5) disrupting the prevailing wisdom.

Committing to Change

Social change is impossible without a deep commitment to a particular cause. However, as much as advocates of social change talk about the characteristics of entrepreneurs and other actors, they rarely address the two qualities (virtues, beliefs, values) that seem central to commitment: (1) purpose and (2) perseverance.

Purpose and perseverance are deeper than the usual characteristics associated with successful entrepreneurship. There are reams of research asking whether entrepreneurs are somehow "superior people," as Scott Shane shows in his 2008 book on the illusions of entrepreneurship, but the field is still unsure what "superior" means.

> Entrepreneurs are typically seen as wiser, more insightful, more creative, more initiative, more persistent, more honorable, more optimistic, more resourceful, and more achievement oriented than the rest of us. The myth of entrepreneurship associates "good" characteristics with entrepreneurs and more modest characteristics with the rest of us, so we think entrepreneurs are "better than average" people. But are these myths accurate?

Shane says no, as do many of his colleagues. Despite the thirst for some great variation, the evidence is muddy at best.

The next question is whether Shane's conclusion applies to social and business entrepreneurs alike. The answer may depend on the attributes under review. Instead of focusing on characteristics such as risk taking, creativity, and resourcefulness, perhaps the differences reside in purpose and perseverance.

Purpose. Purpose is central for driving change of any kind, be it through social entrepreneurship, safekeeping, exploring, or advocacy. But social change appears to require a very special purpose: a sense of personal outrage and empathy about the state of the world, and a passion for, even love of, justice, equality, tolerance, freedom, and stewardship of the world's great resources.

Purpose is often defined as a personal mission statement, an amalgam of motivations to change the world, and even a spiritual calling. However defined, purpose provides the answers to the three central questions involved in challenging the prevailing wisdom. First, why have I chosen this path? Who am I serving in this quest for change? And what must I do to achieve impact? The answers to these questions guide the entire journey to a new prevailing wisdom. Purpose always remains the centering force of change.

It is one thing to acknowledge the presence of purpose, but quite another to explain it. Where does it come from, and how does it influence social change? Is it rooted in the personal trauma Lynn Barendsen and Howard Gardner found among their small sample of social entrepreneurs? Is it built upon a spiritual connection to a higher power? Is it a form of social motivation such as the need for achievement? Is it more deeply ingrained in a sense of why we exist at all? Whatever the base, purpose provides the energy to take the very first step toward challenging the prevailing wisdom.

The questions are no doubt challenging, but difficult to answer. Everyone seems to understand that purpose matters, but purpose is a controversial subject, especially in a secular world divided by polarized debates about faith-based work. But this does not mean purpose is irrelevant to social change. It just means we take it for granted, and leave the discussion to each change agent.

The John Templeton Foundation is ready to call attention to the question through its program on beliefs and social virtue. Its support for basic research on character development and the role of beliefs in social virtue provides the opportunity to drill deeper into this core concept. We know purpose is essential; now we need to define, nurture, and strengthen it.

Perseverance. Perseverance is the second deep component of commitment. Perseverance not only increases the odds of success, but it also addresses the disappointments that every change agent faces along the path to impact. Just knowing that one has done everything possible to succeed provides strength under duress and perhaps humility during success. Thus does perseverance produce more perseverance.

If perseverance is so important to entrepreneurial success, the question is where perseverance comes from. Does it reside in deep personality traits such as physical strength or the need for achievement? Is it embedded in the "moments of obligation" that Ashoka and the Echoing Green Foundation believe spark action? Is it a consequence of believing that anything is possible? Or is it even the product of what some might call love?

On Optimism. The central predictor of perseverance appears to be simply optimism. Optimism may flow from deeper personality traits and early experiences, but it appears to be the most visible resource for sustaining action. This notion is well-supported in recent research showing that roughly one-third of independent inventors continue to spend time on their projects after being told they will fail, while almost two-thirds continue to spend money. Other research shows that business and social entrepreneurs have a basic sense of the inevitable. Not only are they highly tolerant of risk, but they have few regrets about past decisions and rely on purpose to generate forward motion. They get tired and dispirited, but continue despite the odds against creating a new prevailing wisdom. In a word, they are audacious, even to the point of hubris.

There is even evidence that optimism comes in different sizes. Summarizing 25 years of research, Frederick and Erinn Crane argued in 2007 that successful entrepreneurs are optimistic, goal oriented, and persistent. In particular, successful entrepreneurs tend to be both "little" and "big" optimists: "Little optimism involves specific expectations about positive outcomes such as finding a convenient parking spot in a crowded shopping center. Big optimism deals with larger and less specific expectations such as believing our economy is on the verge of tremendous growth."

This research suggests that little and big optimists can also be small and big pessimists. Thus, it is the combination of little and big optimism that produces the perseverance, or fortitude, that may ensure success. Successful entrepreneurs do not suffer from unrealistic or destructive optimism, the Cranes wrote: "In fact, the literature demonstrates that successful entrepreneurs are not high-rolling gamblers, and do not delude themselves or distort reality."

If perseverance is built on optimism, the next question is what drives optimism. My past research suggests that four personal values underpin engagement in social change. Simply asked, what are the central facets of commitment? Based on the work leading to my 1998 book *Sustaining Innovation*, the answer is integrity, trust, honesty, and, most important, faith.

Integrity. Integrity involves a deep personal alignment around purpose, and is the central component of inspirational leadership. It is often revealed in the personal discipline and courage required to stay on course. Simply asked, does the commitment to change reside in a personal willingness to sacrifice, make tough choices, and remain centered on the mission despite the turbulence, resistance, and setbacks encountered en route to impact? Defined as an unwavering application of purpose to day-to-day operations, integrity forms at least part of the "ethical fiber" that many define as essential to social change.

Integrity does more than center the leader. It also drives an organization's culture. Integrity provides the courage to push authority downward, lower the barriers to internal collaboration, encourage full participation, prime the organization for innovation, accept new ideas, and drive the call for change all the way down the hierarchy and out into the community. Organizational integrity also involves readiness to create the conditions for others to succeed, even when they do not reside inside the organization. Integrity provides the strength to engage in common cause, withstand inevitable setbacks, and create the momentum to change the world.

Trust. Trust is essential for risk taking and is based on raw experience. It can be deeply grounded in rigorous analysis and tightly linked to past lessons learned, but sooner or later, every change involves a decision to trust a given choice. If change agents have been disciplined about their work, there should be relatively few surprises as they make each decision.

Trust expresses itself in many ways. It helps change agents withstand the second-guessing that often accompanies their decisions; it gives them the courage to celebrate success and even have fun; and it permits them to stand behind their choices as they face into the winds of impact. Change agents need not be great prophets to lead their organizations beyond the so-called zone of the possible. But in doing so, they need to trust their judgments. No matter how much cost-benefit analysis their organizations pour into its decisions, no matter how many evaluators and auditors it brings to each task, change agents must trust their instincts. And that requires trust in their ideas.

Trust must also involve a willingness to admit human frailty. Trust, and the delegation that goes with it, is essential to maintaining a balanced life. Change agents must not sacrifice all semblance of a normal life, and must pay attention to their own physical and emotional health. Change agents work in challenging, stressful environments, and experience plenty of organizational pressure. Not everyone will have the temerity to stand up to the prevailing wisdom and articulate an alternative future. Trust gives them the underlying strength to continue their long march to impact.

Honesty. Honesty involves a metaphorical willingness to look in the mirror, meaning a commitment to measuring results, open conversations about organizational performance, and honest admissions about success and failure. And, for change agents of all kinds, honest dialogue involves knowing when to say yes to a particular intervention, and why to say no to innovation for innovation's sake.

Change agents should only give permission to fail if failure is an option, for example. Similarly, they should only ask for dissent when they are ready to hear it. The key question is how organizations handle the first few mistakes and dissent en route to change. If the first mistake is greeted with fury, it will likely be the last risk the organization sparks; and if the first dissent is met with censorship, it will likely be the last dissent the organization hears. Listening is a two-way street—honest dialogue means keeping the door open for those who have something unpleasant or contrarian to say.

Faith. Faith is at the very center of perseverance. It is based on a sense that there is something bigger than the self. Faith is not rooted in known experience or empirical facts. Rather it is built on a belief that change involves a leap into the unknown and the risk involved. As such, faith often involves a belief that there is a helping hand, a larger force, and even unflinching protection somewhere beyond the change itself. Faith is an activator, comforter, and sustainer.

Faith does not involve religious beliefs per se. Rather, it involves a connection to some higher power. It can be activated by a walk in the woods, a climb to the top of a mountain, a moment of meditation and connection, even a prayer to some unknown force. Whatever the source of strength, my interviews with hundreds of change agents over the past 20 years strongly suggest that this connection is at the core of ultimate perseverance. Asked what helps them keep going day after day of small steps forward, change agents often talk about their basic belief that good work is somehow protected. Simply put, change will occur. They repeatedly say they draw on something much deeper than optimism.

Are they deluding themselves, simply reassuring themselves that they are not alone, or are they right to believe in a source of inevitability? It is anyone's judgment that is often left to theologians. But change agents draw on it in the lonely moments of doubt. They make leaps of faith after all. These leaps may draw on evidence, organizational capacity, and networks of friends and colleagues, but they are leaps nonetheless.

Mapping Assets and Obstacles

Each stage of the social breakthrough cycle draws upon emerging insights about how social breakthrough occurs. Addressing urgent threats appears to be nearly impossible unless we address the obstacles to social breakthrough embedded in assets such as basic freedoms.

Without crossing some minimum threshold on these assets, it is not clear that the other stages of the impact cycle can even begin. Parenthetically, it might also be useful to imagine roadblocks in the arrows that lead from initial assets to commitment and so forth; after all, that is what the prevailing wisdom does to frustrate change. At a minimum, the absence of key assets raises the cost of social breakthrough to prohibitive levels. Why bother igniting an effort if the first move invites a bullet?

Indexes of the condition of assets are one way to improve the targeting, agitation, aggregation, and disruption involved in change. Such an index might focus on the five assets mentioned earlier that seem to matter most for ignition:

1. Public demand for action.
2. The willingness to engage.
3. The basic freedoms for impact.
4. Institutional responsiveness.
5. The capacity for faithful execution of change.

Not only do such assets precede action, but they can be targets for change, too. Indeed, many organizations such as

Amnesty International, Freedom House, and the World Bank are hard at work doing just that. In trying to improve these assets, these and other organizations improve the odds that all other stages of the impact cycle can flow more smoothly.

Most nations, including the United States, rarely achieve maximum levels of every asset. Therefore, we need more research on which assets are necessary *but not* sufficient for social breakthrough, not necessary *but still* sufficient for impact, necessary *and* sufficient for impact, or neither necessary *nor* sufficient for impact.

Moreover, these assets can also be products of social breakthrough. It is perfectly reasonable to suggest, for example, that freedom of the press and greater government transparency are both reasonable goals for reform. They are certainly goals of social entrepreneurs and advocates in the former Soviet Union and China; social entrepreneurs are constantly inventing new ways of sharing information; private companies such as Google and Go Daddy are challenging China's censorship; and journalists continue to risk their lives by defying intimidation, including Russia's Anna Stepanovna Politkovskaya, who was assassinated on October 7, 2006.

Measures of Governance. The best work on measuring the assets for change has involved a veritable industry of social explorers such as the World Bank, Freedom House, and the Bertelsmann and Ibrahim foundations. These indexes have developed strong reputations for effort and outcome, and offer helpful insights on the assets for change.

Most of these indexes are concerned with good governance. Although the term captures many of the assets needed for change, most measures of good governance specialize in one of two areas: basic freedoms (Freedom in the World) or corruption

(Global Corruption Barometer). Both are important to social breakthrough, but do not tell the whole story.

As with any index, every attempt has its strengths and weaknesses. In general, however, the index industry has suffered from several challenges well summarized in a 2007 paper by Daniel Kaufmann and Aart Kraay, both of whom have been deeply involved in building the World Bank's World Governance Index:

- Measurement error is pervasive in all efforts to measure governance and the investment climate.
- Competition within the index industry can reinforce the search for a single, and likely unachievable, silver bullet index.
- The links from governance to development outcomes are complex.

According to Kaufmann and Kraay, there must be more transparency about the actual components of competing indexes, including full disclosure of margins of error, methodologies, and the potential biases of experts and citizens: "Our major theme is that since all governance indicators are limited in various ways, it is important to recognize and exploit the complementarities between alternative approaches to measuring governance." A summative index drawing on the best indicators from across the index industry might be the wisest next step.

Types of Accountability. The major indexes clearly vary in their sources and methodologies, a source of great debate within this branch of social exploring. But they also vary in their overall views of accountability. Several focus on what I have called *compliance accountability*, meaning a focus on adhering to the rules, both broad and specific, of good governance, while others focus on *performance accountability*, meaning a focus on the outcomes, again both broad and specific, of good governance.

However, my sense is that none addresses what I call *capacity accountability*, meaning the basic infrastructure for good governance. As I wrote in *The Tides of Reform*, my 1997 book on 50 years of U.S. government management reform, the three forms of accountability involve very different targets for addressing the assets of social breakthrough.

A compliance-based system seeks accountability through enforcement of clear rules for behavior and is generally measured after the fact. In turn, a performance-based system seeks its impact through incentives for faithful performance, and is measured both during and after the fact.

In contrast, a capacity-based system seeks its impact by measuring the skills, tools, and motivation needed for high performance, and is generally measured before the fact. The tools of production, such as human capital, are the primary inputs; advocacy and stewardship in providing adequate resources are the primary activities; a well-equipped, trained, and motivated public service is one output; and a healthy infrastructure for impact is another output. Defined as such, capacity-based accountability is based on the ability to produce results. In a sense, capacity-based accountability reduces the need for compliance-based accountability and enhances the plan-do-check-act success of performance-based accountability.

Although these types of accountability are not mutually exclusive, capacity has been largely neglected as a measurement focus. The quality and training of public service workers is a case in point. Rules cannot be implemented if individuals lack the expertise to do so; outcomes cannot be delivered if the technology for simple case management does not exist; and corruption often occurs at the individual level where motivations vary greatly.

Designing an Organizational Home

The core question in designing breakthroughs is how to actually challenge the prevailing wisdom. It is a question that has preoccupied the private sector for centuries. Whether embedded in new or existing organizations, entrepreneurship appears to thrive under certain conditions and in specific organizational cultures.

Designing breakthroughs is both a product of imagination and organizational context. Even as entrepreneurial organizations struggle to generate change, they must also create the conditions to produce a steady stream of new ideas that permeate the inevitable rules that come with growth and transparency.

Effective entrepreneurial organizations often tend to resemble traditional organizations on the surface, but differ in ways not always easy to see. Writing in 1995, Mariann Jelinek and Joseph A. Litterer argued that "much of what makes these organizations entrepreneurial is invisible or misconstrued in traditional theory." Whereas traditional theory focuses on organizational characteristics such as structure, rules, and hierarchy, the two authors focused on organizational behaviors such as shared management, "mindful alertness to anomalies," and "superior capabilities of ambiguity absorption." In short, the entrepreneurial species may look very similar to the traditional species but must behave very differently in creating pattern-breaking change.

Even when they are not the source of radical ideas, existing organizations are still involved in the process of change. As my New York University colleague William Baumol argued in 2004, organizations tend to specialize in incremental improvements in radical change, thereby avoiding the risks of revolutionary change, while advancing its cause by polishing breakthroughs.

According to Baumol, small, independent firms imagine and invent, while large firms modify and scale up. "The two types of activity are complementary, in that together they contribute more to growth than either could by itself," he wrote. "The one dreams up and inaugurates the breakthroughs, while the other contributes crucial improvements to performance. . . . The innovative process is indeed implicitly a partnership between the small entity and the large, between David and Goliath, and, in this case, both emerge victorious, and the economy gains a victory as well."

Baumol is no doubt right to emphasize the incremental change that large firms often produce through alliances with new, small ventures. The literature on corporate entrepreneurship suggests that these David-and-Goliath partnerships can also emerge in large firms that create the new, small ventures inside. These large entrepreneurial organizations must be both David and Goliath simultaneously—a balancing act that can produce the breakthroughs needed to solve pressing social problems.

As already noted, existing organizations may be quite capable of launching change, but they are also quite capable of destroying it. Nevertheless, the two types of organizations and activities are complimentary, Baumol writes in his 2004 article. "The one dreams up and inaugurates the breakthroughs, while the other contributes crucial improvements to performance. . . . The innovative process is indeed implicitly a partnership between the small entity and the large, between David and Goliath, and, in this case, both emerge victorious, and the economy gains a victory as well."

Ideas may share the same developmental process in new and existing organizations, but face very different challenges in the two settings. New ventures have greater advantages at the start of the developmental process, while existing organizations have greater strengths as ideas expand.

New organizations are much better in creating a singular vision of change, for example, and can move quickly in developing new ideas that can achieve results, accelerating those ideas toward implementation, and creating growth. They may face greater barriers to sustained impact, particularly given scarce resources in a highly competitive funding environment, but new organizations are particularly good at spotting opportunities for impact.

In turn, existing organizations have special advantages further up the development curve, particularly in providing the resources for scale-up, ensuring sustainability, and stimulating new ideas beyond the original innovation. They may face more obstacles at the start of the entrepreneurial process, but existing organizations have greater strengths, perhaps, in moving a good idea from conceptualization to full-blown diffusion and success.

The overall development process may be similar in new ventures and existing organizations, but the challenges in the two are not always similar. The key challenges for new ventures come later in the process as they move toward scale-up: sustaining, succeeding, and imagining anew. The key challenges for existing organizations come early in the process: imagining, start-up, and acceleration:

- Whereas new ventures are sparked by imagination, existing organizations usually start their change efforts by convincing potential entrepreneurs to act, whether through the creation of skunk works, businesses within businesses, or powerful idea generators that encourage free thinking about the components of change.

- Whereas new ventures drive persistently toward launch, existing organizations must invest resources in protecting new ideas from internal opposition to change. New ventures frequently suffer from what one researcher called the "tall poppy syndrome." Change agents often keep their heads down lest they attract too much attention, largely because the tall poppy that rises above the field is cut down first.
- Whereas new ventures have enormous energy for growth, existing organizations must integrate entrepreneurial risk taking into their prevailing culture, oftentimes by changing the culture itself through a wrenching process of reform. These patterns suggest that existing organizations can learn a great deal from new ventures as they embark on their journey to pattern-breaking change. This journey is fraught with risk, however, and by low survival rates driven in part by the growing that occurs in ripe fields.

In turn, new ventures can learn a great deal from existing organizations as they grow toward impact.

- Whereas most existing organizations already have the scaffolding of production, new ventures must build their structures from scratch as they reorganize themselves for growth. The flat hierarchies that helped them imagine and create must be expanded to include new accountability systems, stronger boards, and risk management. But even as they add new organizational structure, they must remain ever young. As Drayton argued in 2006, "It is appropriate to have a manager come in to run a franchise or manage the 13th department store in a chain, implementing a formula. A little tweak here or there will make the difference in the business's margin. But that is not what fundamental entrepreneurship is about."

- Whereas most existing organizations already have the resources for sustaining momentum, even if they are unable to generate significant market share for several years or more, new ventures have very thin margins for maintaining momentum, often devoting huge amounts of time and energy to fund-raising and social enterprise (revenue generation) in an effort to provide a floor to continue their endeavors.
- Whereas most existing organizations already have experience with tracking systems, new organizations usually face great difficulty creating meaningful measurement systems, in part due to the costs and potential delays in action. This pressure often produces a paradox: Young, new organizations often lack the resources, measurement, and agility to imagine new paths to impact, while old, large organizations have the resources and measurement, but not necessarily the commitment to act.

Both new and old organizations alike share a similar concern about resources. Both sets of organizations also share the overriding need to maintain an entrepreneurial orientation over time. To the extent they copy existing organizations in the world writ large, even the most entrepreneurial venture can develop organizational sclerosis, especially if it spends too much time admiring the large, old organizations that dominate the Fortune 500.

By focusing on what Drayton calls the "entrepreneurial quality," social-benefit organizations in any sector can move away from the debate about newness as an institutional attribute and toward a much more productive debate about maintaining the commitment to change over time. It does not matter where proposals come from, but rather where they go.

Aggregating Pressure

Social entrepreneurship exists as a critical driver for creating social breakthrough. However, there are times when a new combination of ideas will be irrelevant for a new prevailing wisdom. Social entrepreneurship must take its proper place as a form of agitation that leads directly into aggregation for social breakthrough.

Social impact networks are highly fluid collections of individuals and organizations that work together to challenge the prevailing wisdom and disband soon afterward. As such, social breakthrough networks resemble the hazy breakthrough networks that Hugh Heclo first introduced in 1978 in describing policy coalitions built on ever-shifting sand.

A *breakthrough network* is best defined as a loose partnership of interest groups, lobbyists, policy entrepreneurs, legislators, presidents, bureaucrats, and agencies banded together for a successful legislative siege. In contrast to the old-fashioned "iron triangles" that protect the conventional wisdom through tight links between the bureaucracy, interest groups, and congressional committees, breakthrough networks exploit relatively short-term opportunities for creating change.

Visualizing Breakthrough Networks. Breakthrough networks have several characteristics that play a prominent role in their formation and impact. First, they are mostly temporary—they have been described as "coalitions in the sand." Members come and go as compromises are made; some join with each new piece of a bill; others are bought or rented with a campaign contribution or funding for a pet project; still others pull away as their positions are eroded.

Second, there is rarely one issue in a given policy space. There might be one aligned against disruption, for example, and another in favor of action. Although networks exchange members as the policy process moves forward or backward, there may be multiple networks and nodes of contact. A single member, usually an alliance or major interest group, may bring a group of allies to a network, while other members may join as individual entities.

Third, it follows that members of most networks are loosely coupled. Again, unlike the iron triangles that prevent change and enshrine the prevailing wisdom through tight connections between members of the status quo, breakthrough networks are easily fractured, rearranged, and dissolved as the environment changes. By definition, iron triangles are highly stable and can align against breakthrough networks. As breakthrough networks begin to roll forward, iron triangles often block action—that is why they are called iron, after all.

When most of us hear the words "social breakthrough," we think of nonprofits. But nonprofits are not the only organizations that produce social breakthrough. Nor are they the only players. As the following list suggests, social breakthrough networks can contain dozens of actors, many of whom have what Drayton described as "the freedom, confidence, and societal support to address any social problem and drive change."

- Evangelists (e.g., faith builders).
- Engagers (e.g., citizens, petitioners).
- Congregations (e.g., broad coalitions, communities).

- Entrepreneurs (e.g., innovators, inventors, engineers).
- Visionaries (e.g., highly visible leaders, goal setters).
- Early adopters (e.g., beta testers).
- Truth tellers (e.g., researchers, contrarians, op-ed writers).
- Exemplars (e.g., heroes, role models).
- Power brokers (e.g., political parties, investors, candidates).
- Hidden hands (e.g., "kitchen cabinets," board members).
- Campaigners (e.g., lobbyists, public interest groups, coalitions).
- Bundlers (e.g., organizers).
- Bridge builders (e.g., blenders, movement builders).
- Strategists (e.g., planners, pollsters, engineers).
- Muses (e.g., dreamers, hope makers).
- Jugglers (e.g., multiple role players).
- Investors (e.g., foundations, donors, governments).
- Enterprisers (e.g., fund-raisers, revenue generators).
- Architects (e.g., capacity builders, mentors, consultants, network designers).
- Translators (e.g., sense makers, explainers, interpreters).
- Mappers (e.g., issue crawlers, matchmakers, recruiters).
- Deciders (e.g., policy makers, members of Congress, presidents, elites, influentials).
- Implementers (e.g., rule makers, frontline employees, practitioners).
- Monitors (e.g., reporters, bloggers, Facebookers, tweeters).
- Educators (e.g., teachers, professors, trainers, coaches).
- Historians (e.g., writers, storytellers).

These actors come and go with the ebb and flow of opportunities for impact. They enter the breakthrough cycle as social entrepreneurs, social safekeepers, social explorers, and/or social advocates, and work together toward social breakthrough.

Although breakthrough networks sometimes disband with the rise of new prevailing wisdom some actors always remain engaged in protecting past breakthroughs, which are almost always under duress. Having created both traditional coalitions and novel connectors through the new media, they build a sum-greater-than-the-parts, achieve their desired social breakthrough, disband, and move on to other issues.

These networks are often composed of unexpected and unfamiliar partners such as lobbyists, pollsters, and strange bedfellows of one kind or another. In 2010, for example, hedge funds became heavily involved in promoting charter schools in New York State. No one is quite sure why, but the *New York Times* reported in April 2010 that lifting the state's cap on the total number of charter schools has become a cause célèbre for hedge fund philanthropists and their political action committee. "A lot of hedge fund and finance people in New York had decided state politics was too dirty, and focused on their philanthropy," said Boykin Curry, a partner of Eagle Capital Management. "I think there's an awakening now that we can be a force in Albany, but we've got to play a tougher game than before."

Given the enormous range of allies available for agitation, breakthrough networks require at least some coordination to succeed. However, as Figure 3.2 shows, networks are inherently complex, and evolve over time as they build, expend, and deplete assets.

A Breakthrough Network at Work. The recently created Partnership for a Healthier America is a good example of a breakthrough network under construction. It is being built by six organizations—the California Endowment, Kaiser Permanente, Nemours, the Robert Wood Johnson Foundation,

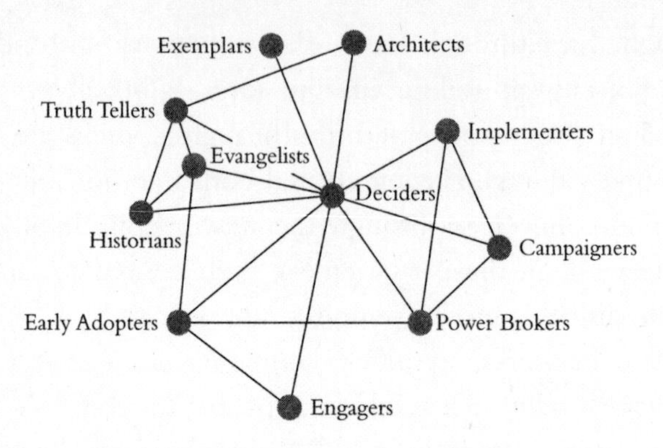

Figure 3.2 An Illustrative Breakthrough Network

the W.K. Kellogg Foundation, and the Alliance for a Healthier Generation, itself a small network forged by the American Heart Association, William J. Clinton Foundation, and Robert Wood Johnson Foundation. It also has a strong partner in the federal government's new interagency task force on childhood obesity, which was created under presidential memorandum with all the associated fanfare.

The Partnership for a Healthier America has a single goal: "Raise a Healthier Generation of Kids." The mission statement is simple, sharp, and highly focused on impact. Its strategy is clear, too:

- Developing a strong membership network of leaders across sectors with commitment to scaling meaningful and measurable solutions.
- Convening members annually to affirm, align, and announce commitments.
- Promoting broad understanding among all sectors about the role healthy food, physical activity, and the environment play in reversing the childhood obesity epidemic.

- Facilitating and measuring the impact of members' commitments against clear and transparent targets.
- Connecting potential partners in the private and nonprofit sectors to each other and to the correct points of contact in government to ensure efficient leveraging of actions, and sharing of knowledge and lessons learned at the community, state, and national levels.

The strategy blends all four elements of social breakthrough. It is built in part on the social entrepreneurship that has brought Whole Foods into poor urban neighborhoods such as North Philadelphia; the social safekeeping that has protected and expanded past breakthroughs such as food stamps, now called the Supplemental Nutrition Assistance Program (SNAP); the social exploring that has generated a deep inventory of research on what causes obesity, perhaps most notably including the Robert Wood Johnson Foundation's Commission to Build a Healthier America (which, in the interest of full disclosure, I evaluated on the foundation's behalf in 2009); and aggressive social advocacy.

Its primary spokesperson is none other than Michelle Obama, who had been working on the issue with dozens of partners for more than a year before launching the partnership on February 9, 2010. "The physical and emotional health of an entire generation and the economic health and security of our nation is at stake," the First Lady said. "This isn't the kind of problem that can be solved overnight, but with everyone working together, it can be solved. So, let's move." Sounds like an urgent threat to me.

Some might argue that the network is built around such a feel-good issue that it cannot fail, but the problem has been worsening for decades, in part because we have long failed to recognize that health involves more than health care, as my friends at the Robert Wood Johnson Foundation would point out.

This network could not and will not succeed without the full participation of all players—no single entrepreneur, defender, explorer, or advocate will be enough. There is no room for a boutique funder or change agent looking for a gold star. Almost by definition, networks diffuse credit to all participants.

Disrupting the Prevailing Wisdom

Breakthrough networks do not exist in isolation—they operate in a dense environment of support and opposition. As Duke University's Paul Bloom and Gregory Dees argued in a 2008 article, social breakthrough occurs within an ecosystem that contains many paths to success. Although they focus on social entrepreneurs, their message clearly applies to breakthrough networks as well:

> To understand and change these social systems, social entrepreneurs should borrow insights from ecology and use an ecosystems framework. Long ago, biologists discovered the limits of studying living organisms in isolation. Biologists gain a much deeper understanding only by considering the complicated relationships between organisms and their environments. They look not only at the social breakthrough that environmental factors such as soil and water have on organisms, but also at the social breakthrough that these organisms have on one another and their environment.
>
> Human societies are just as complex as ecosystems, with many different types of players and environmental

> conditions. Management scholars have recognized the parallels between biological and economic systems. Recently, researchers in the field of strategic management have focused greater attention on the parallels between biological and organizational systems, even adopting the phrase *ecosystem strategy* to refer to an approach for guiding a breakthrough network's strategic choices. Proponents of an ecosystems framework stress the value of understanding the complexity and dynamics of the wide-ranging forces a breakthrough network faces.

Given this complexity, it is no surprise that there are dozens, if not hundreds, of tactics involved in change. According to Gene Sharp, for example, there are at least 198 tactics of nonviolent action, including Lysistratic nonaction (withholding sex) and the satyagrahic fast (Mahatma Gandhi's notion of fasting as a way to sting the conscience of the adversary). However, as Sharp explained in his 2003 book, the list is only a starting point for moving toward social breakthrough:

> Without a doubt, a large number of additional methods have already been used but have not been classified, and a multitude of additional methods will be invented in the future that have the characteristics of the three classes of methods: nonviolent protest and persuasion, noncooperation, and nonviolent intervention. It must be clearly understood that the greatest effectiveness is possible when individual methods to be used are selected to implement the previously adopted strategy. It is necessary to know what kind of pressures are to be used before one chooses the precise forms of action that will apply those pressures.

The challenge, therefore, is to focus networks on clear strategies for bringing pressure to bear on an issue such as health care, inequality, hunger, or disease. Consider two of the newer approaches to both effecting change and preparing for action: (1) swarming, and (2) effects-based planning.

Swarming. Networks come in many shapes and sizes. Some operate through a single node that exercises tight control of all network members, while others involve networks of networks that are loosely coupled as actors compete against each other for credit and funding even as they cooperate to achieve impact.

Whether simple or complex, networks are particularly effective when they swarm a specific target. According to the 1998 book by David Ronfeldt, John Arquilla, Graham Fuller, and Melissa Fuller, swarming involves a "deliberately structured, coordinated, strategic way to strike from all directions at the same time." It works best, they argue, when designed around the coordination of widely dispersed "pods" that are organized into "clusters" to carry out a multifront attack. Developed as a new tactic for war fighting, swarming has actually had its most recent test in social breakthrough.

Although wars will still be found with huge armies and large maneuvers, swarming is becoming the preferred method for both social and military revolution. From 1994 to 1998, for example, Zapatista rebels in Mexico used swarming to mount a social revolution in the southern state of Chiapas. Although their revolution started on January 1, 1994, as a traditional military conflict between relatively small fighting units, the Zapatista forces eventually switched to what the *New York Times* called "the first postmodern revolution."

The revolution relied on a virtual battle built upon a breakthrough network composed of human rights groups such as Amnesty International, Physicians for Human Rights, the Jesuit Refugee Service, and Food First to come to its cause through the Internet. What began as a traditional war of bullets soon became a war of e-mails, faxes, and coordinated pressure. As the swarming increased, the Mexican government collapsed into chaos, foreign creditors panicked, and the international community rallied toward a peaceful resolution of the conflict. Although the Mexican army could have easily destroyed the Zapatista forces, the information "netwar," as Ronfeldt et al. called it, brought the government to the negotiating table only 12 days into the conflict, and again each time the war flared back up. The effort to disrupt the prevailing social equilibrium was carefully targeted and coordinated, and was supported by an infrastructure that deployed resources effectively.

Effects-Based Planning. It is one thing to give breakthrough networks a long list of possible tactics, and quite another to give them the tools to "focus fire" on an intended effect. Moreover, some negative effects may be simply unavoidable.

The effort to help breakthrough networks create intended effects has produced some of the RAND Corporation's most promising recent research, including much of its work on creating more accurate "ensembles" of possible futures. It has even prompted Paul Davis to imagine what he calls "a grand challenge for the analytical community" in thinking about effects-based operations as a core operating principle of a high-performing military. Despite its heavy focus on military success, the method is relevant for almost any organization interested in creating impacts, be it in the arts, education, or health, or in government, business, or the nonprofit sector.

According to Davis, an effects-based operation starts with a basic commitment to "mission-system capability." This capability refers to what he calls "the no-excuses ability to accomplish missions under a wide range of operational circumstances and to characterize the range of circumstances for which the capabilities are sufficient to provide different degrees of confidence." As Davis might ask, what must breakthrough networks possess to succeed in a variety of settings, and how does additional capacity either add or subtract from that capacity?

Anchored in advanced mathematics and modeling, RAND's effort to advance the research on effects-based operations is often esoteric. It is also clearly rooted in what Davis labels "the revolt of the war fighters," including the young Air Force officers who were appalled by "the frequently mindless and ineffective use of air power in Vietnam. . . . When their turn to lead came, they were determined to do better. The Gulf War was their first great opportunity, and, in fact, joint fires (not just Air Force fires) were applied with decisive effectiveness as the result of sound thinking about affecting *systems*, not just servicing targets."

It is also driven by the "revolt against standard models and analysis." As Davis readily admits, "Most modeling and analysis still encourages a mechanistic view of warfare that emphasizes firepower and attrition while ignoring other critical aspects of strategy, such as maneuver of forces and fires, command and control, and aspects that relate to each side's effort to attack its opponent's strategy, will, cohesion, and cognition—as in a drive for decision superiority." Substitute the words *sales, manufacturing, and services* for the word *warfare*, and you have a nice summary of the current frustration with academic research on organizational life.

The notion that breakthrough networks should develop plans based on what Davis calls the "direct, indirect, and cascading effects" of each option makes perfect sense. The only challenge is to make sure that all the effects and their uncertainties are fully vetted. Although Davis might well take offense at the idea of an informal version of effects-based operations, especially given his deep commitment to modeling, the ethos of the method is applicable across almost every aspect of organizational life. Wars are not the only events that take place in complex systems that are mysterious and hard to predict.

Building a Robust Breakthrough Cycle

Participants in the breakthrough cycle have never been under greater pressure to anticipate the future, yet have never had so many futures to anticipate. They no longer face a single future or two against which to plan, but hundreds, if not thousands, of plausible futures, some laden with opportunity and promise, others filled with threat and risk.

The proliferation of plausible futures has increased the importance of uncertainty as a variable in network performance. Although change agents can fight the uncertainty by hoarding resources and hunkering down against opportunity, 50 years of research by RAND indicates they would be better off hardening themselves against uncertainty by building links that can bend and flex against many futures and counterattacks.

The network must remain alert to the potential collapse of vulnerable assumptions as circumstances change, agile in hedging against these vulnerabilities, adaptive in altering both what they produce and how they operate, and always aligned around a clear mission. Networks do not change for change's sake but are able to do so when it is warranted. In a word, they are robust.

Robustness is a term well-known to engineers, mathematicians, and even coffee roasters, but it has yet to gain much traction in the field of organizational studies, where the term *resilience* has much more currency in describing a breakthrough network's ability to bounce back from crisis and attack. According to *Merriam-Webster's Collegiate Dictionary*, being robust means "having or exhibiting strength or vigorous health"; "having or showing vigor, strength, or firmness"; "strongly formed or constructed: sturdy"; "capable of performing without failure under a wide range of conditions"; "rough, rude"; "requiring strength or vigor"; "full-bodied"; and "hearty."

In sum, a robust breakthrough cycle is resilient. It is able to bounce back from an external shock and/or the breakdown of key assumptions about the futures participants face. And, contrary to calls for maximum efficiency, participants in a robust breakthrough cycle build redundancy and flexibility into their management systems.

Searching for Robustness

Based on my three-year study of the RAND Corporation, which was published in 2005 as *The Four Pillars of High Performance*, robustness resides in the ability to exploit an opportunity with the right intervention at the right time. "If you look at a little start-up company, then they're likely to bet the whole company on a single future," said James Dewar. "If you look at a multinational, then maybe they'll do robust decision making across 90 percent of the company, while the other 10 percent takes a flier and hopes that some of those will pay off. I just don't think of a little start-up company as being agile or very alert. They're just going to build whatever they want to build and hope it works."

Robustness is often revealed in periods of high turbulence, largely because existing strategies continue to work reasonably well during periods of relative calm. According to RAND's Robert Lempert, robust organizations excel when the environment changes quickly or dramatically: "That's when the organization that cannot implement robust adaptive plans may fall behind. I am thinking of the observation that many private-sector firms that are market leaders in some dominant technology fail to make the leap when a disruptive technology comes along. The organizations can't change rapidly enough to adapt to the new world."

In the short run, the participants in a robust cycle may actually underperform against their opponents, if only because they keep at least some of their capital in reserve to hedge against surprise. They may also look less innovative than their peers, if only because they may be less willing to bet the company on a single breakthrough. In the long term, however, a robust breakthrough cycle should produce higher growth and more innovation, if only because it protects itself against vulnerability by moving quickly to exploit new opportunities for agitation, aggregation, disruption, and breakthrough.

Building Robustness

It hardly makes sense to adopt a robust plan if the participants in the breakthrough cycle do not have the alertness, agility, adaptability, and alignment to adjust to uncertainty. The issue here is not whether an organization or sector is robust per se, but how much robustness it can muster against an uncertain world. The same issue applies to social breakthrough cycles.

Alertness. Participants in the breakthrough cycle cannot hedge against vulnerability and exploit opportunities unless they can see the changing futures ahead. However, staying alert does not mean collecting piles and piles of data.

Instead, RAND would generally recommend that participants of all kinds create signposts that might reveal a change in the validity of a given assumption about a market, competitor, product, or supply chain, or an increase in the vulnerability of such an assumption. Changing validity simply means the company was wrong about some future condition, while increasing vulnerability addresses the growing weakness about a particular assumption that might mean the difference between success and failure.

As noted in the previous discussion of social exploring, RAND has invented a number of tools that participants in social breakthrough can use to increase their effectiveness and targeting, even as they anticipate and hedge against the breakdown of critical, load-bearing assumptions underpinning an operating plan.

Some of these breakdowns involve surprises, while others are the product of forks in the road such as global warming and new unthinkables such as pandemics and global economic collapse. But whether the breakdown involves surprise or long-term vulnerabilities, the key to alertness starts with a landscape of possible futures against which to plan, and continues with an honest assessment of what has to go right for nothing to go wrong and what cannot go wrong for a plan to go right.

Agility. Participants in the breakthrough cycle must act quickly when their assumptions break down. Having discovered a potential flaw or collapse rooted in surprise and uncertainty, they must rally and redeploy resources such as personnel, supplies, logistics, and dollars to strengthen or change the foundation of their load-bearing assumptions. As Winston Churchill wrote of Great Britain's victory in the long-forgotten 1899 Sudan River War, "Victory is the beautiful, bright-colored flower.

Transport is the stem without which it could never have blossomed." His quote applies to all stages of the breakthrough cycle, too.

Agility also involves deep concern for the mundane world of logistics, supply chains, and virtual command structures that can move anywhere, anytime. The same might be said of any social breakthrough. Yes, there are great heroes; yes, there are great battles; and yes, courage is essential, as well as a good battle plan. But if you can't get the supplies in the right hands at the right time with the right tools, you're not going to succeed. I believe that supply-chain management may have as much to do with ridding the world of malaria as the vaccines we are working to develop. No vaccine, no vaccination.

Adaptability. *Adaptability* is not just another synonym for a new round of innovation. As an attribute of robustness, it is best defined as the ability to rapidly adjust tactics and/or strategies to meet vulnerabilities and opportunities as signposts of emerging futures reveal them. Sometimes, adaptability will demand true innovation—original, disruptive ideas that challenge the prevailing wisdom in a field; other times, it will involve incremental adjustments in an existing plan. Innovation is a form of adaptability, but not all adaptability involves innovation.

Alignment. Breakthrough cannot occur without a tight alignment around the many participants in the breakthrough cycle. Participants must constantly remind each other of the overall destination, create metrics for assessing success, and reinforce incentives for driving strategy downward and across their organizations and networks.

RAND's leading researcher on military recruiting, James Dertouzos, explains alignment as a merger of goals and incentives.

His current research suggests wide variation in how military recruiters respond to relatively small changes in their recruiting goals. As he explains: "We're getting estimates that suggest people's effort can decline by as much as 20 percent just because their mission is unachievable. They essentially give up. I don't know whether it's a morale issue or whether it's responding to incentives in a very calculated way or what. When missions are not allocated appropriately either over time or from market to market, you get these incredible diminutions in observable effort. You can gain 10 to 20 percent gains in productivity in certain markets by just aligning markets and incentives."

Given the onslaught of urgent threats, it is no wonder that networks are mulitplying. Although concerned with innovation and social breakthrough, they must also build the core infrastructure to manage the enormous uncertainties they face.

Exploiting Punctuations

Past research on business entrepreneurship often focuses on waves of creative destruction that come and go over time. These waves pulse through the economy in what researchers call long waves, rising and falling away as a new equilibrium forms and stabilizes. Breakthrough networks certainly help create punctuations, but they must also be ready to take advantage of opportunities that arise during certain periods of time such as the Great Society in 1964, which produced a massive list of breakthroughs.

These long waves also appear to exist in the public policy process, which is more relevant perhaps to the discussion of social entrepreneurship. "The common core of policy agenda research," Frank R. Baumgartner, Christopher Green-Pedersen, and Bryan D. Jones wrote in 2006, "is attention to the dynamics of how new ideas, new policy proposals, and new understandings of problems may or may not be accepted in the political system. . . . New issues or ideas may well meet resistance from the prevailing political arrangements, but they sometimes break through to create dramatic policy changes."

According to Baumgartner and his co-authors, such breakthroughs reflect a "disjointed and episodic trace" of policy activities that build over time. "As new participants with fresh ideas break into the inner circle of policy-making, the system is jolted; there is nothing smooth about the process of adjustment in democratic societies."

In short, the opportunities for big social change often arise during punctuations in time, and tend to close relatively quickly as the policy system either realigns around the new ideas or musters the support to reject them. This cycle of destruction and potential rejection was unmistakable in 1987 to 1989 when Congress first provided a breakthrough catastrophic health benefit for Medicare recipients, then abolished it two years later under pressure from the American Association of Retired Persons.

This conclusion fits well with Bill Drayton's 2002 argument that innovation is not a common event: "Innovation typically comes in waves. A big, pattern-change innovation triggers years of follow-on change as the innovation is adapted to more and more social and economic sub-sectors and spreads geographically. This dynamic is one of the reasons leading social entrepreneurs are so critical." Robust breakthrough networks must be ready to act when these opportunities arise.

Conclusion

The breakthrough cycle is not just about aggregation of pressure. It is about producing change through whatever means possible. Some of this change will come from social movements, strategic alliances, and catalytic collaboration. But whatever the tactic, the concept is clear. The breakthrough cycle has enormous potential for addressing urgent threats, but has often been stalled by the search for the one in 10 million that Drayton believes might lead the world out of chaos.

I believe the greatest obstacle to an effective, fast-moving cycle is the desire for credit, whether by individual leaders, organizations, or funders. Were there mythic heroes involved in the great breakthrough cycles of the past? The answer is absolutely yes. Gandhi, King, Reagan, and Obama (both Barack and Michelle) were undeniably exceptional. But they also understood that they were part of something bigger than themselves, and that change involved assets, commitment, new and old ideas alike, and more.

All were willing to share credit widely. Having watched major breakthroughs come and go, it is often impossible to identify the single leader or funder that made it all possible. Credit had to be diffuse, if only to protect the network from the collapse or withdrawal of a single node built around a specific set of actors.

We cannot become so obsessed with the heroic leader that we forget the power of networks. Could civil rights have reached the boiling point without Martin Luther King Jr.? The answer is almost certainly no. Was he absolutely essential? The answer is almost certainly yes, though the expansion of civil rights to include women, the disabled, those at the end of life, and gays and lesbians moved forward with other leaders and networks. Moreover, the history of civil rights shows that King focused on building and expanding the breakthrough network for major legislation and new social norms. Massing, swarming, pulsing, strategic events, marketing, and political pressure were his tools. These tools still exist today. They might be a bit rusty, but it is time to take them out again.

Chapter 4

Prepare to Expect Wonders

Putting all of the definitional debates about social entrepreneurship aside, today's challenge lies in both creating and protecting the world's great breakthroughs for solving the urgent threats ahead. It hardly matters who does the work if it gets done.

Doing so involves new tools for understanding the future and creating tightly anchored ideas for impact. We cannot suppose that a particular program will work, not without intense scrutiny and instant access to data. We must prove our point, define our theories of impact, provide hard data, establish high social rates of return, and be honest with ourselves about what does and does not work.

We also need the courage to cooperate. Social entrepreneurs, safekeepers, and advocates all have plenty of energy and creativity to bring to a new equilibrium. They also have plenty to say to the powers that be about what communities need, how programs work, and where we must invest, and plenty of muscle both to achieve and defend social breakthroughs.

After all, our goal is not winning an award, although winning one is part of celebrating success and drawing young Americans into the breakthrough cycle. Rather, our goal is social breakthrough and new, stable social equilibrium that Roger Martin and Sally Osberg described so well.

Where We Have Been

The field of social entrepreneurship is expanding rapidly, and occupies a central role in the search for what works in social change. Endorsed by the president and backed by modest federal resources, many of the nation's best-known scholars and practitioners are involved in the effort.

As they work toward expanding the field, these actors are confronting the basic definition of terms. There is less concern today about the hard definition of terms, though, and greater concentration on how to build the field toward sustainable breakthrough. This shifting focus reflects a new concern about how to bring new combinations of ideas to scale, not just by building bigger organizations such as Teach for America and the Knowledge Is Power Program (KIPP), but also by encouraging collaborative creativity and catalytic collaboration to aggregate the agitation fostered by young, new entities.

This shift reflects a growing awareness that new combinations of ideas may not be enough to address the urgent threats on the horizon. We need to move faster if we are to tackle poverty, inequality, hunger, global warming, and intolerance fast enough to alter the prevailing wisdom. This sense is clearly motivating the field toward more aggressive work on social impact, built on the notion that social entrepreneurship can occur anywhere in a society, whether through celebrated 24/7 organizations or moderately entrepreneurial existing agencies, as well as through individual or collective action. With the Obama administration in office, there is also a growing awareness that power matters greatly to ultimate impact. Just as Ashoka measures its success in part through policy change, the field is starting to build measures of durable impact, which include the astute use of power.

The field is also starting to embrace the basic principle that social entrepreneurship comes in several forms, including what I have labeled Type A and Type B entrepreneurship. It also involves more ecumenical networks of social safekeepers, explorers, and advocates. Either social entrepreneurs must broaden their organizations to include these skills, which will take time and scarce resources, or they must abandon their search for distinctiveness. The fastest way to get these skills is not necessarily through traditional visions of the supersized organization, but through the acquisition of expertise from other partners with similar interests. There is no need to duplicate the capacity that already exists outside the field's boundaries. Driver follows purpose, after all.

Defined as such, the new social entrepreneurship erases the artificial boundaries that divide the field among researchers, actors, disciplines, and alternative paths to impact. It might be titled "Social Change in Four Flavors." Not only are there different types of social entrepreneurs, but there are also different drivers that produce change, including traditional civic organizing. We cannot become so concerned with igniting new combinations, however important they might be, that we ignore the many ways that those ideas produce change.

Nor can we become so focused on one driver that we ignore the great breakthroughs that are steadily being eroded or the infrastructures that both create and protect achievement. We cannot let past breakthroughs wither through neglect or complacency, not to mention the kind of cozy relationships and bureaucratic breakdowns that produced the Gulf oil spill. Creating social change involves more than creating the new combinations of ideas, important though they are in sparking breakthrough—it also includes the aggressive safekeeping of what we have already achieved. This protection involves more than simple defense. It also involves a good deal of offense. We cannot let the business model of entrepreneurship delude us about the odds of long-term success.

This long-term success involves aggressive investment in the infrastructure of change. It is no surprise that such investment might flag during periods of economic distress and budget cuts. But these are poor excuses for letting the infrastructure decay. We must maintain and rebuild our core institutions, especially at a moment when so many essential organizations are coming apart. Although we do have good news on this front through the new $50-million infrastructure fund being deployed by Grantmakers for Effective Organizations, there is much more to do. We cannot continue with occasional investment in the undergirding of effectiveness.

Where We Should Go

Imagine for a moment that homeless shelters were no longer full beyond capacity, food pantries no longer understocked, and life-threatening diseases such as HIV/AIDS, malaria, cholera, and tuberculosis were finally eradicated. The resources we invest in social breakthrough could be put to use on new challenges and needs instead of being stretched to the breaking point by a tsunami of economic havoc. We pay special attention to new threats and counter pressure from the old equilibrium. There are great incentives to maintain inequality for sure, and "fortune at the bottom of the pyramid" exists in large measure because there actually is a bottom of the pyramid. We must keep the focus on change no matter what the barrier and never relax.

Encourage Engagement

There are many ways to make a difference toward social breakthrough, whether voluntary, low-intensity work such as a weekly durable commitment to any social-impact organization or voluntary, high-intensity work such as a career in any sector (no sector has a first-refusal right to talent these days—students should go where their talents will be best used). Contrary to the conventional wisdom embedded in days of service to commemorate events such as September 11th (which was a lead item in the Serve America Act), episodic engagement may do more harm than good. Social impact requires perseverance even if in the form of an hour a week. There is room for everyone in social breakthrough. We are all leaders now. It is a critical lesson learned.

Embrace Power

We have to give power its due. Changing the prevailing wisdom is not for the faint of heart, especially when power comes into play. We have to become more comfortable using the term, while learning how to apply it effectively. I do believe in the power of a good idea such as palliative and hospice care, but the health care bill contained precious little on the issue, in part because the existing equilibrium at the time distorted the concept in its campaign against so-called death panels. A bit of power would have helped.

Breakthroughs need not involve conflict, however. There are issues such as the 2009 expansion of AmeriCorps that involve bipartisanship and cross-sector collaboration. But there are times when we must take a stand and confront sharp divisions. Social impact will always involve the threat, if not reality of battle—we may try to resolve our differences peacefully, gracefully, but there will be times when we have to fight. We have to find the physical, emotional, and spiritual reserves to keep going in spite of the inevitable resistance and setbacks we will encounter.

Nor is bipartisanship an enemy of change. There are always opportunities for compromise, although some undermine the integrity and honesty that underpin perseverance. However, we cannot be so astutely nonpartisan (dare I suggest because our funders demand it for their own protection?) that we ignore the role of power in achieving results. We can be nice but tough; friendly but agitated; ecumenical but unyielding. There are times for compromise in pursuit of change, and times for hardball. We must be able to take a punch and equally willing to give one.

Support Exploring

We must embrace the social exploration needed at every stage of the social breakthrough cycle. Researchers can certainly make a difference by celebrating success and studying failure, informing the current generation of entrepreneurs and teaching the next, and testing hypotheses and debunking myths.

But researchers can be a force for good only if they let the evidence take them where it will. They must confront the field with hard questions about its assumptions, tough analysis of the facts, and a readiness to speak truth to power. No matter how much they might believe in one assumption or another, and no matter how much they want to be invited to celebrate the great potential of social entrepreneurship, researchers must maintain enough distance to make sure they focus on what they know, not on what they hope.

Researchers must also resist the temptation to tell the field what it wants to hear. By their nature, researchers are contrarians. They are at their very best when they confront the prevailing wisdom to prove it right or wrong. In a very real sense, they must be part of the continuous upset that moves a field forward—not so much through the creative destruction that renders entire industries obsolete, but through a readiness to challenge the dominant theories that are too often used to explain success and failure after the fact. They must use their own entrepreneurial qualities to help the field advance on solid evidence. Bluntly put, they must persevere when the prevailing ideologies of social breakthrough push back.

Innovate Naturally

We must make social change easier. It does not have to be a highly individualized struggle against the odds. Social impact can be life-threatening, of course, especially when it involves authoritarian tactics by governments or civic groups. But we can make social breakthrough easier through relatively small investments in the social infrastructure. We cannot be so consumed with the idea of change that we arm ourselves with antiquated systems, tactics, and ignorance.

Building a robust breakthrough cycle is not an accident. It is built piece by piece to emphasize the alertness, agility, adaptability, and alignment needed for success. Ignore one element and the odds of failure increase; ignore a second, and the odds of failure reach near certainty. The same holds for the organizations that occupy the infrastructure of change.

I remain particularly concerned about the durability of 24/7 heroism, if only because of the physical and emotional toll it takes. Much as I admire the new heroes of social breakthrough, we must create an appropriate balance between the single-minded pursuit of a vision and the need for high-performance management. Working 24/7 without enough staff to succeed is a recipe for turnover and pause.

Working 24/7 can also be dangerous to one's health. Change agents are expected to persevere without pause, sometimes without a living wage to support them. It would be no surprise if they exhibited high rates of physical and emotional duress that go with pursuing their vision. If investors want to sustain high rates of engagement, they must be willing to invest in the entrepreneurs who provide it, which means the administrative support (including pensions, a living wage, and health insurance) to pursue social breakthrough. Even heroes need rest once in a while—it is not a badge of honor to turn in unused vacation time each year.

Celebrate History

We must honor and protect the past. We need everyone engaged in the current movement to solve great problems, and we must always respect and honor the change agents who created the great breakthroughs that now need protection. They built the platforms for today's endeavors, the opportunities for imagining third ways for impact, and the frameworks, laws, and practices that we now seek to expand, fine-tune, and protect. We must not become so concerned with distinctiveness and awards that we forget what already works. Where is the award for durable social safekeeping? Exploring? Advocacy? The number of nominations would be overwhelming but well worth considering.

Rebuilding the Infrastructure of Change

There has never been a greater need for a new prevailing wisdom. The world has faced many urgent threats before, but today's list of problems seems to be growing faster and accelerating to tipping points that leave little room for reversal. Even as these threats advance, old breakthroughs are collapsing under economic pressure, partisan counterattack, and complacency.

The temptation is to throw every resource at the threats, using so-called top kills and junk shots to slow and solve seemingly intractable threats. But many of the urgent threats will take decades to solve and may require fundamental changes in human behavior. Without a durable infrastructure to support the new and old combinations of ideas, it is not clear that breakthrough can be sustained long enough to succeed. As I wrote in 2008 in *The Search for Social Entrepreneurship*:

> Given the promise involved in the general movement toward altering a persistent and resistant social equilibrium, the field needs to be much more supportive in helping social entrepreneurs achieve their goals, whether through organizational development, renewed infrastructure investment, more aggressive research and development, stronger networks of other social

> entrepreneurs and socially entrepreneurial organizations, [or] further encouragement and funding of management improvement.

This infrastructure of change enables virtually everything that leads to social breakdown. Measured at any given point in time, infrastructure is an output of basic organizational activities such as raising money; forging partnerships; organizing work; recruiting and training board members, leaders, and employees; generating ideas; managing budgets; and evaluating programs. Once created, these resources are consumed in mission-related program activities such as treating patients, feeding the hungry, building housing, producing art, educating students, training workers, and so forth. Once expended, they are regenerated through the same organizational activities that created them in the first place.

Unfortunately, persistent disinvestment in the social-impact infrastructure is putting many past and future breakthroughs at risk. This is why we need infrastructure builders, translators, and promoters who can make the case for investment such as the *Nonprofit Quarterly*, Nonprofit Finance Fund, the *Stanford Social Innovation Review*, the Edna McConnell Clark Foundation, and a host of other teachers, mentors, trainers, consultants, coaches, and translators.

There is little doubt that the infrastructure of change has eroded with the continuing jobless recovery from the 2008 economic catastrophe. The U.S. Congress seems unable or unwilling to strengthen the faithful execution of the laws, even as evidence mounts of systemic breakdowns in the implementation and maintenance of past breakthroughs. At the same time, the infrastructure of change is being cut everywhere possible, mostly in the overhead activities that support success in all aspects of entrepreneurship, safekeeping, exploring, and advocacy.

The social-change infrastructure is clearly under stress, but its future is still uncertain. Will it miraculously survive largely intact? Will it waste away to a largely ineffective destination for social change? Will it put agitation on hold as it fights to survive? Or does it have choices about how to use the current crisis to its advantage?

Consider four landscapes of the future that face the infrastructure as the social, economic, and political environment are buffeted by polarization. These landscapes are built on a set of general assumptions regarding relatively low public confidence, suppressed giving and tax revenues, the U.S. government's 5 percent discretionary spending cutback, and increased demand for virtually every service created by past and current breakthroughs on urgent threats such as health care. The question, as Ebenezer Scrooge might put it, is not whether any one future will be, but which future will emerge. Will the infrastructure choose its destiny? Or will it allow the future to take its course without pushing back?

The Miraculous Rescue

The first scenario might be called "the miraculous rescue." The basic assumption is that Americans are a generous people and will continue giving, perhaps rising to the challenge and giving more from their increasingly meager coffers. There is some basis for this behavior in the American psyche, which includes the empathy that drives generosity and outrage that creates the demand for change. However, the amount of new giving that might emerge in the wake of calls for greater investment à la Bill Gates and Warren Buffett could easily be offset by declining government, corporate, and individual giving. It could be a simple displacement effect—more private giving could ease the conscience and sympathy that drives private giving.

Even if it did occur, this rescue would likely help some nodes in the infrastructure but not others. The public is aware of and used to supporting certain types of groups but not others. There are whole fields of work that receive little in private donations because they have traditionally been subsidized so heavily by government.

These are often virtually unseen by the public, and many of them also work with the most vulnerable and sometimes scorned of populations—the chronically mentally ill, developmentally disabled, and substance abusers. Some of these programs are quite intensive; some are residential and therefore, expensive. Many such programs are funded through the state and will be subject to the trickle-down effect of reduced federal budgets combined with reduced tax income at the state level.

As for a national or international bailout, the prospects are dim, especially given the growing concerns about the sovereign debt crisis. Some well-known organizations did receive stimulus support, even as the American Red Cross received the first of what could be several visible bailouts in winning a $100-million no-strings grant from Congress following hurricanes Gustav and Ivan. But these rescues came at the beginning of the economic calamity, and are now running out.

The Hollowing

The second scenario might be called "the hollowing." It is much more dispiriting but more probable. Most infrastructure organizations, even ones with nationally known brand names, have been affected by the downturn. In the social-benefit sector, for example, annual fund-raisers and galas have fallen well short of past highs, even as once-steady gifts are shrinking. Several major corporate foundations have stopped giving entirely, particularly in the beleaguered financial sector, and many have trimmed back to near zero. Government is also looking at deep deficits and will adjust nonprofit contracts accordingly.

Depending on the duration of the jobless recovery and declining government revenues, many infrastructure organizations will starve themselves into a weakened organizational state through hiring freezes, pay freezes, layoffs, and deferred organizational maintenance. Large infrastructure organizations are not immune to these cuts—expect at least one or two brand names to take draconian measures to stay afloat. How ironic that an infrastructure created in part to help the needy may well contribute hundreds of thousands to the ranks of the nation's unemployed. Federal job centers remain overwhelmed by demand as roughly 20 million Americans are now looking for help. How many of these individuals will be from the infrastructure of social change?

The Arbitrary Winnowing

The third future might be called "the arbitrary winnowing," and is based on the collapse of many smaller social change organizations. Although the Internal Revenue Service recently reported that it certified almost 60,000 new tax-exempt organizations in 2009, it also reported that it has no way to count the number of closures. Some infrastructure organizations, particularly those that are entirely dependent on individual or government funding, will go under, while others will prosper as contributions flow to the most visible and largest organizations, as well as to those most connected to their donors, which in some cases may be their communities.

Marketing budgets and community support may be the best predictors of survival—well-managed organizations will survive through more aggressive fund-raising appeals, while midsize organizations with little immediate capacity to replace lost funds will falter and cut to the bone. Some small infrastructure organizations will survive through sheer will or because their communities are used to supporting them, others will merge or be acquired, others will simply melt away, and still others will be mothballed for better times in some distant future.

Taken to an extreme, this random winnowing would effectively crush the small organizations at the bottom of the infrastructure, while creating fewer but bigger organizations at the top. This will have much the same effect that the merger-and-acquisition fury of the 1980s and 1990s had on the private sector and airline industry. Overall employment will fall somewhat, though not as deeply in some areas of the country, but the total number of social-change organizations could drop by 10 percent over the next decade.

At least for now, this winnowing will have a random effect across the sector as some infrastructure organizations exit, while others hang on with minimal staffing and budgets. As with the hollowing scenario, this winnowing will undermine the sector's ability to meet increasing demand, especially among smaller infrastructure organizations rooted in the communities hardest hit by the recession.

The Great Transformation

The final scenario might be called "the great transformation." This fourth scenario is hopeful but not well formed two years into the deepest recession in modern history. Moreover, fundamental transformation is both expensive and difficult. Are there services that must be saved over others in state budgets? Lobby for that scenario. Are there ways to reconsider the design of our organizations to achieve greater synergy between community players? Are there ways to involve our communities in rethinking and reenergizing our work? Transformation will require deliberate and collective action by the sector's stakeholders—communities, funders, governments, intermediaries, constituents, nonprofit associations, and boards.

The Need to Act Wisely

It is still too early to know which of these futures will come true. Social-change organizations can still choose their future, however, which should provide at least some hope that the infrastructure of change can yet be rescued from a long recovery.

At least to date, there has been more hollowing out than miraculous rescue, winnowing, or transformation. Most social-change organizations have already gone through one downsizing and some have gone through two. Reserves are being exhausted where reserves even existed. Credit lines are tight. And the economy is still in the cutting phase.

Think of the overall infrastructure as a kind of bureaucratic pyramid with many more employees at the bottom than the top. Just like the federal government over the past 50 years, the social-change infrastructure is becoming more like a pentagon with many more employees at the middle than the bottom. Some of the reshaping is through attrition-based downsizing, while some is driven by the steady accretion of needless bureaucracy. The infrastructure seems to be convinced that more layers and leaders per layer create stronger leadership. In fact, the opposite is true.

The hollowing largely occurs at the bottom of the social-change infrastructure through attrition-based downsizing—we simply leave the empty jobs vacant. But quit rates, as we call them, are much higher at the bottom than the top of the hierarchy. By leaving jobs vacant, we reduce our ability to deliver core services, which creates a vicious circle in periods of increased demand accompanied by ever-weaker infrastructure. Volunteers can take up part of the slack, but it's difficult to put a volunteer into a complex job, especially one that requires deep training, on-the-job experience, and continuing education, not to mention government certification.

Past research from the Nonprofit Finance Fund suggests that the first victims will be organizations that depend on government funding. They have lower reserves and higher accounts receivable. In other words, they operate with slimmer margins than many other types of infrastructure organizations even in the best of times and, of course, state and local governments are imposing significant payment and contracting delays, which puts pressure on credit lines and reserves.

The random hollowing of the sector produces a simple table comparing value and vulnerability. Ideally, the hollowing would affect the least valuable organizations, be they vulnerable or not. But as Table 4.1 shows, it is not always clear whether the creative destruction of the sector is occurring in the right place. Much as funders and advocates may believe in social Darwinism, the current hollowing appears to be random at best and pernicious at worst.

Table 4.1 Strategies for Thoughtful Hollowing

	Valuable	**Not Valuable**
Vulnerable	Invest	Ease out
Not Vulnerable	Scale hold steady	Merge or close

Mundane though it might seem, this is a time for building a robust infrastructure based on agility, alertness, adaptability, and alignment. This is not an agenda just for social entrepreneurs. It is for social-breakthrough networks as a whole. Without a commitment to a robust infrastructure, we may look back on this period as a great wave of neglect that blocked our path in this age of urgent threats.

Scaling to Impact

Social change demands strong organizations. Although the infrastructure is a sum greater than its organizations, improvement starts at the bottom of the pyramid with individuals and their organizations.

Paul Bloom and Brett Smith made this point in the March 2010 inaugural issue of the *Journal of Social Entrepreneurship*. Writing about the need to improve the research base on scaling social entrepreneurship, the authors focus on seven forms of organizational capacity that ebb and flow over time for growth and/or impact. This SCALERS model offers important insights on refining the velocity and vector of change:

1. Staffing: the organization's ability to recruit and retain talent, whether they are senior executives, midlevel managers, frontline employees, or volunteers.
2. Communicating: the organization's effectiveness in persuading key stakeholders that its change strategy is worth adopting and/or supporting.
3. Alliance building: the organization's strength in building and maintaining partnerships, collaborations, joint ventures, and networks for social change.
4. Lobbying: the organization's capacity to advocate for policy action that produces big change.

5. Earnings generation: the organization's expertise in generating a stream of revenue that exceeds its expenses.
6. Replicating: the organization's success in replicating the programs and initiatives that it has originated.
7. Stimulating market forces: the organization's commitment to creating incentives for encouraging partners to pursue private interests while serving the public good.

This model is particularly useful for measuring organizational capacity over time. If Bloom and Smith are right, these several forms of scaling capital should rise as organizations drive toward higher performance. The stronger they get, the more they can contribute to social change. The model is also quite relevant for measuring the more general capacity of sectors and social networks. All need the same capabilities.

It would be naive to argue that the "organic" organizations discussed in the following pages can become "reflective" organizations overnight, but it is possible to accelerate the injection of needed capital to move them upward more quickly. After all, there is no speed limit on capacity building. At least for now, however, most social-change organizations are on their own as they struggle to create SCALERS forms of organizational capacity. Although some funders such as Ashoka do provide high-quality consulting, and some such as the Skoll and Edna McConnell Clark foundations provide large grants toward organizational capacity, most organizations remain on their own as they try to master the journey to social breakthrough.

The High-Performance Organization

Imagine the journey to high performance as a climb up a spiral staircase with five major "landings" or stopping points along the way: (1) the organic landing where change agents struggle to create a presence in their environment; (2) the opportunistic landing where they scale toward impact through growth and fine tuning; (3) the intentional landing where they focus more tightly on what they do best; (4) the robust landing where they strengthen their infrastructure against uncertainty; and (5) the reflective landing at the top of the spiral where they address longer-term issues of succession and legacy.

The journey up this spiral is anything but predictable. Some social-change organizations linger at one landing or another waiting for more funding, new leadership, or a strategic plan; others squander past successes as they change directions with the latest fad; and still others reach the reflective step of full, robust impact only to discover that they have no purpose left.

This image of a developmental spiral comes from the 25 case studies that were featured in my book *Sustaining Nonprofit Performance.* The 25 organizations were part of a much larger sample of high-performing organizations nominated by members of Grantmakers for Effective Organizations (GEO), the Alliance for Nonprofit Management, and the Association for Research on Nonprofit and Voluntary Action (ARNOVA), but were hand picked for the range of their impact and the variety of missions.

The list included large organizations and small, young organizations and old, but all were engaged in significant social change. Some were still at the beginning of the process, while others had already made their mark on a new prevailing wisdom. Eight of the 25 organizations had budgets under $1 million when I visited them in 2001–2003, another seven had budgets from $1 million to $10 million, and 10 had budgets over $10 million. There were four that were both young (seven years or less) and small (under $1 million); five were young but larger (over

$1 million); four were middle-aged (between 7 and 15 years old) and small; two were middle-aged and larger; and 10 were older (more than 15 years old) and larger.

Like most social-change organizations today, these 25 organizations continue to face an uncertain future. It is not clear what might happen to the global economy as debt increases; how far societies will go in reversing past breakthroughs; and whether the next generation of change agents can survive complacency and attack. What is clear is that change agents must master the developmental spiral to solve the world's toughest problems.

The question here is not whether social-change organizations can achieve high performance during times of turbulence, however. They can and do. Nor is it whether they can create miraculous effects in spite of internal flaws. Again, they can and do. Rather, the question is how to move more organizations up the developmental spiral toward sustainable high performance described below.

The Organic Organization. Whatever their ultimate goal—be it to end poverty, feed the hungry, alter public policy, or produce great art—every social-change organization starts with the same simple goal: to exist. I believe the most important questions are asked at this very first landing: How will we make a difference? Who does what in the organization? How will we govern ourselves? How will we know we are successful, if we are? The answers must be found if the organization wants to create early momentum toward social breakthrough and must be asked frequently if the organization is to claim any purpose but survival.

Organic social-change organizations face inevitable trade-offs between passion and caution. If start-ups had to wait until their programs and systems were perfect, they would never launch at all. Yet if they launch without asking hard questions about their ability to deliver on the promises they make, they almost certainly will disappoint or disappear. They must be visible enough to attract support while creating the capacity to produce results. This often involves difficult choices and trade-offs for organic organizations. Friends of the Chicago River, an environmental advocacy group incorporated in 1988, faced this investment dilemma. Asked whether he thought start-ups should first work on management or on their program, a senior executive said, "It's a constant juggling act of nurture this here, nurture that there. It takes a lot of skill to develop strong programs without having the management stuff in place. You have to operate a lot by intuition, which can put you in harm's way."

Growth eventually provided the resources for long-overdue investment. "In the beginning years, our bookkeeping and administration were really a mess," this executive explained. "We all agreed that if we had to slip on something, it was going to be on certain types of paperwork. We waited until we could afford to take those on, until our programs were stronger and people were saying, 'Wow, you guys are doing a lot of great work.' Then we could say, 'Now we have to fix up our infrastructure a little bit.'"

Unfortunately, some organizations never leave this landing in large part because they never test the load-bearing assumptions that support their basic program goals—for example, whether the world will behave as they hope. Too many also launch without making the basic decisions about tracking results and accounting for time and money. And too many launch without creating basic expectations for governing the organization. Although their leaders must work hard to build identity, these young organizations must outline the internal infrastructure that will hold them together as they confront a turbulent, competitive environment. This means investing in simple reporting routines, clarifying board and staff responsibilities, and building basic operating systems, all of which respond to simple capacity-building interventions.

The Opportunistic Organization. Assuming that they garner enough support to grow, many organic social-change organizations advance to the opportunistic step, where they promptly get stuck. Having achieved enough credibility to compete for resources, opportunistic organizations face a number of challenges as they seek to expand their attack on the prevailing wisdom. Some find it nearly impossible to say no to the funding they need to survive, while others branch out into fields well beyond their original program intent, and still others become the hot organization that attracts early funding. But what goes up in the enterprising step often comes crashing down when the next new thing shows up.

There is nothing wrong with stretching the organization into what I call the "zone just beyond possible," particularly if the organization is making a measurable difference through its work. But the stretching can create confusion, underinvestment in core administrative systems, and employee burnout as the organization tries to meet all the deadlines it has accepted. Having started out with a clear sense of direction, opportunistic organizations often evolve into multiservice agencies that have drifted far from the core mission they once embraced.

Growth is not harmful if it takes a social-change organization where it wants to go, however. Organizations have a better chance of getting where they want to go if they have a careful map of their environment, if innovation fits with their program goals, and if their leaders work to reconcile new initiatives with the old. They are also much more likely to expand gracefully if they have the measurement and tracking systems to know where they are at any given point in time and what they did to get there. This means investing in more elegant analysis of environmental threats and opportunities, internal organization, board and staff development, and measurement, all of which respond to capacity building.

The most significant differences up and down the spiral involved strategic planning. Although almost all of the 25 organizations had a strategic plan, the enterprising-focused organizations clearly devoted more energy to the effort. If not quite a fear of planning at the opportunistic and focused steps, there were definitely concerns about costs, readiness, and implementation. Simply put, some of my intentional and focused organizations worried that they simply could not afford to plan.

Opportunistic organizations face the challenge of planning for the future while dealing with the day-to-day complexities of running an organization. Much as they want to be strategic, opportunistic organizations have to be tactical to survive. For example, one interviewee said, "When your organization is in rescue mode, a strategic plan is kind of nice but won't fix your problems. It is like you want to be flying at 30,000 feet, but you're stuck on the ground." Another commented, "If things are bleeding, it is not the time to look five years in the future. You have to figure out if you are going to survive until tomorrow."

The Intentional Organization. Opportunism has its costs, of course, not the least of which is the erosion of purpose and clarity. Driven in part by survival, many opportunistic organizations change their programs to meet the latest request for proposals, often expanding their mission with each opportunity. It is only through genuine review of mission, priorities, threats, and true mission-centered opportunities that these organizations can rise from opportunism to intention.

Becoming intentional often involves a confrontation with the dependencies created during the opportunistic phase, particularly for organizations that grew by stretching well beyond their original program goals. Often, organizations can become more intentional only through downsizing, restructuring, a new board, and a change in leadership, all of which increase the organizational capacity to invest in the activities they care about most.

Letting go requires a return to the basic purpose of change and the core values of perseverance. Intentional organizations can face intense board and employee resistance, as well as a community backlash. They may find it difficult to reassign employees who were hired for their specialized skills, nearly impossible to combine units with very different program histories, and intensely stressful to spend scarce resources on organizational infrastructure. Intentional organizations often discover that each of their enterprises has its own language and culture, and they almost always conclude that streamlining, reorganizing, downsizing, and focusing are easier said than done.

Organizations that move from the opportunistic step to intentional action take a hard look at everything. As a senior executive at the Nature Conservancy told me in 2002,

> The challenge is to stop doing things that we've always done that are not contributing toward the mission. The first step is to use "zero-based planning" and take a fresh look at everything we're doing. We're not going to get rid of people, but we are going to change what people do. We would like to grow from 3,000 people to 10,000, but we want the 10,000 to be doing the right things and have everything aligned so they have the incentive to do the right things.

The move from opportunism to intention does not have to be done alone. It is often done through mergers and strategic alliances with other organizations that are also spread too thinly or through expansion in a particular line of work. It is also often done with the support of a community foundation or venture philanthropy that is ready to commit resources to a more focused future. Such investments are rarely made without the underlying evidence to show program results and organizational productivity, however. To the extent that intentional organizations set high expectations for evidence and adopt ever more sophisticated systems, they raise the odds that they will attract the energy, if not the funding, for the next move upward.

The Robust Organization. Once at the intentional step, social-benefit organizations often take steps toward focused action. Simply defined, robustness involves "the ability to withstand, even exploit, uncertainty." All organizations, social-benefit or not, exist in a world of many futures: some favorable, some threatening. Robust organizations prepare for uncertainty by hedging against vulnerabilities and shaping the environment for maximum effect.

At CARE, for example, the global campaign against poverty involved two very different planning efforts. The first dealt with internal structure and systems, while the second turned to the mission itself. "The first strategic plan was more inward looking," a senior executive explained. "That is, we were trying to increase our fund-raising, build up our systems and our structures, and make us more effective within. Programmatically, we had changes going on, but the second strategic plan was much more outward looking. It was more concerned with how we were interacting with the world and what we were contributing to the world rather than focusing inwardly on our structures."

Hedging against uncertainty involves more than fretting about surprises. It requires a basic willingness to think in futures (plural) tense, which, in turn, requires an agile organizational structure, concentration, and insurance against surprises. It also requires a greater focus on the longer term. Robust organizations must be able to run sprints, particularly when reacting to surprises, but their great strength is the marathon.

Unlike the elementary planning that helps organic organizations to test their program assumptions, for example, robust organizations prepare for multiple futures simultaneously. Most set aside at least some funds for the worst case, deepen their insurance against a range of catastrophes, and often create contingency plans for acting quickly to stem the financial damage from cost overruns and surprises such as rapid escalations in health care costs. They build financial systems that operate in real time, meaning that they can get accurate revenue statements at a moment's notice, and often create early-warning systems, or signposts, that show trouble ahead. As they build, robust organizations also engage in basic risk analysis, weighing new program costs against potential benefits.

Robust organizations are perfectly capable of innovation, however. They often take enormous leaps of faith. But those leaps are well informed by careful analysis and measurement. Robust organizations are just as likely to believe in luck as their peers, but they often create the luck they need by building the organizational structure for maximum opportunism. "We all make our luck," said an executive with OMB Watch, a good-government advocacy group. "Or maybe a better way to put it is that we have to position ourselves to seize the opportunity when lucky situations come about. We have to have proposals ready, be ready to engage the policy fights, be ready and knowledgeable about a range of issues. Maybe I'm being cavalier, but the luck comes from other people respecting the work we do. The timing of it is fortuitous, which I call luck."

Much as focus helps organizations cope with uncertainty, it can also breed isolation and hubris. The more focused the organization becomes, the less accountable it can become. It can lose its sense of direction, drift toward imperialism and self-righteousness, and abuse the opportunities that come with independence. Hence, even as they protect themselves against uncertainty and stay lean, robust organizations must continue to challenge and inspire themselves, while investing in basic accountability systems. The more they face into the environment through measurement, formal and informal contact with their markets, benchmarking against other organizations, and strategic thinking, the better.

The Reflective Organization. Once they reach the top of the development spiral, social-benefit organizations confront a dilemma: having achieved a near-monopoly in their field, they must ask whether they are still fulfilling their purpose for change. Instead of seeing themselves as victims of uncertainty and surprise, reflective organizations focus on their own contributions to the future through advocacy, example, and legacy. Some even decide to close their doors to make room for other social-change organizations that are moving up behind them.

Having achieved the independence of adaptability, reflective organizations often return to the organic questions that sparked their initial journey, challenging themselves to merge their present capabilities with their past intentions. They often do so by exploring the future through even more advanced planning techniques such as computer-assisted simulation, streamlining their administrative structures through organizational assessment and staff rotation, preparing for inevitable departures through succession planning, and renewing their management systems through upgrades and innovation.

To me, high performance is always a mix of qualitative and quantitative factors. Expansion just by virtue of doing more programs or having a larger budget is not necessarily a sign of organizational effectiveness or even organizational growth. It can be a measure of failure. The questions to ask are: "What are the qualitative underpinnings behind quantitative growth?" "What are our outcomes as a result of that growth?" "Are we just touching people's lives or are we helping to achieve change in people's lives?" That's the difference. One can greatly expand the number of lives one touches but do nothing else, and that, to me, is not effectiveness.

Absent this self-discipline, reflective organizations can easily become imperial organizations, imposing their will on the rest of the field, while absorbing resources that might better go to other organizations. Not unlike large corporations, they may become so focused on self-preservation that they forget what brought them into being in the first place.

Organizations do not have to be large to be reflective, however. To the contrary, they may be quite small relative to the organizations against which they sometimes compete. They almost certainly act younger, whether by constantly streamlining, incubating new organizations within their own midst, fostering deliberate board and staff turnover, undertaking constant benchmarking against other organizations both inside and outside the field, entering new collaborations and strategic alliances, or contemplating mergers and spin-offs, all of which face the organization in the outside world. Reflective organizations remain reflective in part by revisiting the techniques that helped them to move upward through each landing of the developmental spiral.

Patience as a Virtue

These are tough times for creating and protecting a new prevailing wisdom—budgets are tight, the public has change fatigue, and there is a strong backlash against breakthrough. We need action beyond campaign rhetoric or popular catchphrases that typically lack substance or fail to sustain effort. We also need to confront knee-jerk proposals such as pay freezes and hiring caps, which merely contribute to the problems we seek to solve.

Again, there is no single route to a stronger infrastructure. Most organizations know they do not have the resources they need. They also feel great pressure to deliver the mission even if doing so steadily depletes the resources needed for what some think of as the luxury of capacity building. Why put in a new and expensive information system when a 56K modem still works? Why waste time and energy on strategic planning, a marketing plan, or board development when urgent threats are rising?

Most organizations also know that their infrastructure is rusting. Having interviewed nearly 200 social entrepreneurs for their Common Good report, James Weinberg and Frances Kunreuther of Commongood Careers concluded that social breakthrough had never been more important, but also never more precarious:

> The societal, economic, and political landscape looks very different in 2010 from that which existed just

a few years ago. Faced with a range of new realities, social entrepreneurs feel that they are approaching an *inflection point*, or a moment of dramatic change for their organizations and movement. Despite diminished resources, social entrepreneurs are now working to grow in entirely new ways and at faster rates than ever before.

These conditions and goals are putting incredible stress on systems that were already running at nearly full capacity. To be successful in moving to the next level, leaders need to take the entrepreneurial skills that they used so successfully in programmatic development and focus their talents on enhancing internal operating systems. Organizations need to build capacity, enhance efficiency, and leverage human capital in order to increase their social breakthrough per dollar invested.

Patient capital may be the most important source of needed funding for protecting and rebuilding infrastructure. The Acumen Fund is a leader in applying the concept through its portfolio of investments. According to the Acumen Web site, "Patient capital is understood as a debt or equity investment in an early-stage enterprise providing low-income consumers with access to health care, water, housing, alternative energy, or agricultural inputs. . . . Our aim in investing patient capital is not to seek high returns, but rather to jump-start the creation of enterprises that improve the ability of the poor to live with dignity."

Acumen defines the concept with a simple set of bullets.

- Longtime horizons for the investment.
- Risk tolerance.

- A goal of maximizing social, rather than financial, returns.
- Providing management support to help new business models thrive.
- The flexibility to seek partnerships with governments and corporations through subsidy and coinvestment when doing so may be beneficial to low-income customers.

Unlike Acumen and a handful of other funders, most capacity building comes in small bursts when funders stumble upon a little extra money. But that approach often produces capacity building without foresight or intention.

I vividly remember meeting with a social-change arts organization in Minneapolis that had four grants for strategic planning—one on ballet, another on musicals (big revenue producers), another on the canon, and still another on edgy theater. When I asked which one was the true focus of the theater's work, the founders answered, "None of the above." But the money was malleable—it was being used to cross-subsidize what the theater really did. Five years later, the theater went bankrupt. If only the capacity building had been properly planned, the theater might still be producing some of the best art in its market.

Even with the most thoughtful plan, it costs money to increase productivity, innovation, and transparency. I believe these investments return more than they cost, however. But even if infrastructure costs more than it returns, it is essential for trust, transparency, accountability, and the increased productivity needed for all elements of social breakthrough.

Former Federal Reserve Board chairman and champion of public service Paul Volcker believes it, too. As he argued in April 2010, this is a particularly important moment to push forward on public service excellence: "Public demand for results is high, but confidence remains low; interest in public service of all kinds is clear, but service in the government remains a questioned destination at both the top and bottom of the hierarchy; the need for high-performance government is undeniable, but seems just out of reach when crisis strikes." Speaking of the need for immediate action, Volcker concluded: "A great society deserves no less." His statement applies to every sector involved in social change.

A Final Point

This book is based on the simple premise that social entrepreneurship is a significant source of new combinations of ideas for changing the world. However, as the book argues, social entrepreneurship is neither the only driver in agitating the prevailing wisdom nor always the best choice for addressing urgent threats. As the breakthrough cycle suggests, navigating the ecosystem of change involves many steps, each one of which contains its potential and hazards.

The conversation about social entrepreneurship is clearly moving in this direction as attention shifts toward scaling up promising ideas and achieving durable breakthroughs in solving the world's greatest problems. Early work on social entrepreneurship has led to increased concern about and interest in how to move new combinations toward scale, even as more current work focuses on the new combinations of actors that might assure faster impact. Indeed, one can even argue that social networks are new combinations on their own, a form of social entrepreneurship that occurs at the latter stages of the social breakthrough cycle.

Social entrepreneurship will always be an alluring act, in part because there is such great courage and perseverance involved. But it is not the only source of change—nor would many of its strongest supporters suggest as much. There are plenty of problems on the horizon that demand attention, some of which endure almost entirely because past breakthroughs have collapsed. We already know what to do about many of the problems facing the world, largely because the laws, norms, and practices are already in the statute books, judicial precedents, international agreements, and successes that form their own class of breakthrough. The challenge is not always to create a new combination of ideas; rather, the challenge is to muster the collective courage to create the future even as we defend the past. The industries of deprivation are always waiting, as are their own networks.

It is now time for collaboration. Social entrepreneurship has proven its value and must be given its due. But it must be kept in perspective as but one of the ways to create breakthrough, and social entrepreneurs must be encouraged to join the fight already under way throughout society. If that means partnerships with those ancient legacy organizations that are sometimes pushed aside, social entrepreneurs must join. If that means working with social explorers to monitor the future, social entrepreneurs must listen. And if that means creating grand alliances with social advocates, social entrepreneurs must give ground. Today's battle is not about the one-best-way to change the world, but about creating and harnessing the ordinary heroism across society to create the change so desperately needed in this time of urgent threats.

Indeed, almost all of the great social breakthroughs of the past half-century have been driven forward by a profound commitment to plant the seed of change and help it grow everywhere possible. Henry David Thoreau captured this command in his long-forgotten essay, "The Succession of Forest Trees":

> Though I do not believe that a plant will spring up where no seed has been, I have great faith in a seed—a, to me, equally mysterious origin for it. Convince me that you have a seed there, and I am prepared to expect wonders.

Perhaps this is the perfect definition of how the four drivers of change work together to create a new prevailing wisdom: prepare the world to expect wonders.

Bibliography

I have used many references in this book, but elected not to populate the text with a long list of endnotes. Instead, I have placed the most important resources on the following list. Some are directly quoted in this book, but others form the backbone of my ongoing effort to define social entrepreneurship and other forms of agitation en route to social breakthrough.

Aldrich, Howard E., and Martha Argelia Martinez. "Many Are Called, But Few Are Chosen: An Evolutionary Perspective for the Study of Entrepreneurship." *Entrepreneurship Theory and Practice* 25 (2001): 41–57.

Allison, Graham T., Jr. "Public and Private Management: Are They Fundamentally Alike in All Unimportant Respects?" Proceedings for the Public Management Research Conference, Washington, D.C., November 19–20, 1979. Office of Personnel Management, 27–38.

Alvord, Sarah H., L. David Brown, and Christine W. Letts. "Social Entrepreneurship and Social Transformation: An Exploratory Study." *Journal of Applied Behavioral Science* 40 (2004): 260–282.

Asterbro, Thomas, Scott A. Jeffrey, and Gordon K. Adomdza, "Inventor Perseverance after Being Told to Quit: The Role of Cognitive Biases." *Journal of Behavioral Decision Making* 20 (2007): 253–272.

Audia, Pino G., and Christopher Rider. "A Garage and an Idea: What More Does an Entrepreneur Need?" *California Management Review* 48 (2005): 6–28.

Austin, James E., Howard Stevenson, and Jane Wei-Skillern. "Social and Commercial Entrepreneurship: Same, Different, or Both?" *Entrepreneurship Theory and Practice* 31 (2006): 1–22.

Barendsen, Lynn, and Howard Gardner. "Is the Social Entrepreneur a New Type of Leader?" *Leader to Leader* 27 (2004): 43–50.

Baron, Robert A. "Cognitive Mechanisms in Entrepreneurship: Why and When Entrepreneurs Think Differently Than Other People." *Journal of Business Venturing* 13 (1998): 275–294.

Baumgartner, Frank R., Christopher Green-Pedersen, and Bryan D. Jones. "Comparative Studies of Policy Agendas," *Journal of European Public Policy* 13 (2006): 959–974.

Baumol, William J. "Entrepreneurial Cultures and Countercultures." *Academy of Management Learning and Education* 3 (2004): 316–326.

Baumol, William J. "Entrepreneurship and Invention: Toward Their Microeconomic Value Theory." AEI-Brookings Joint Center for Regulatory Studies Paper No. 05-38 (2005).

Behn, Robert. "Management by Groping Along." *Journal of Policy Analysis and Management*, 7 (1988): 643–663.

Bloom, Paul N., and J. Gregory Dees. "Cultivate Your Ecosystem." *Stanford Social Innovation Review* 6 (2008): 47–53.

Bloom, Paul N., and Brett R. Smith. "Identifying the Drivers of Social Entrepreneurial Impact: Theoretical Development and an Exploratory Empirical Test of Scalers." *Journal of Social Entrepreneurship* 1 (2010): 126–145.

Bornstein, David. *How to Change the World: Social Entrepreneurs and the Power of New Ideas*. New York: Oxford University Press, 2003.

Bornstein, David, and Susan Davis. *Social Entrepreneurship: What Everyone Needs to Know*. New York: Oxford University Press, 2010.

Boschee, Jerr, and Jim McClurg. "Toward a Better Understanding of Social Entrepreneurship: Some Important Distinctions." 2003. Found at www.se-alliance.org/better_understanding.pdf.

Cheng, Yu-Ting, and Andrew H. Van de Ven. "Learning the Innovation Journey: Order Out of Chaos." *Organization Science* 7 (1996): 593–614.

Collins, Jim. *Good to Great: Why Some Companies Make the Leap . . . and Others Don't*. New York: HarperCollins, 2001.

Crane, Frederick G., and Erinn C. Crane. "Dispositional Optimism and Entrepreneurial Success." *Psychologist-Manager Journal* 10 (2007): 13–25.

Crutchfield, Leslie, and Heather McLeod Grant. *Forces for Good: The Six Practices of High-Impact Nonprofits*. San Francisco: Jossey-Bass, 2007.

Cunningham, J. Barton, and Joe Lischeron. "Defining Entrepreneurship." *Journal of Small Business Management* 29 (1991): 45–61.

Damanpour, Fariborz. "Organizational Innovation: A Meta-Analysis of Effects of Determinants and Moderators." *Academy of Management Journal* 34 (1991): 555–590.

Davis, Paul K. *Analytic Architecture for Capabilities-Based Planning, Mission-System Analysis and Transformation*. Los Angeles: RAND Corporation, 2002.

Davis, Susan. "Social Entrepreneurship: Towards an Entrepreneurial Culture for Social and Economic Development." Paper prepared for the Youth Employment Summit, Alexandria, Egypt, September 7–11, 2002.

Dearlove, Des. "Interview: Jeff Skoll." *Business Strategy Review* 15 (2004): 51–53.

Dees, J. Gregory. "Enterprising Nonprofits." *Harvard Business Review* 76 (1998): 55–67.

Dees, J. Gregory. "The Meaning of 'Social Entrepreneurship.'" 2003. Found at www.fuqua.duke.edu/centers/case/documents/dees_sedef.pdf.

Dees, J. Gregory. "The Social Enterprise Spectrum: Philanthropy to Commerce." Harvard Business School Case #9-395-116 (1996).

Dees, J. Gregory, and Beth Battle Anderson. "Framing a Theory of Social Entrepreneurship: Building on Two Schools of Practice and Thought." Presented at the Association for Research on Nonprofit Organizations and Voluntary Action Conference, November 17–18, 2005. Reprinted in *Research on Social Entrepreneurship: Understanding and Contributing to an Emerging Field*, edited by Rachel Mosher-William, 39–66. ARNOVA Occasional Paper Series. Indianapolis, IN: Association for Research on Nonprofit Organizations and Voluntary Action, 2006.

Dees, J. Gregory, and Beth Battle Anderson. "Sector-Bending: Blurring the Lines between Nonprofit and For-Profit." *Society* 40 (2003): 16–27.

Dees, J. Gregory, Beth Battle Anderson, and Jane Wei-Skillern. "Pathways to Social Impact: Strategies for Scaling Out Successful Social Innovations." Center for the Advancement of Social Entrepreneurship Working Paper, August 2002.

Dewar, James, Carl H. Builder, William M. Hix, Morlie Levin. *Assumption-Based Planning: A Tool for Reducing Avoidable Surprises.* Cambridge: Cambridge University Press, 2002.

Drayton, William. "The Citizen Sector: Becoming as Entrepreneurial and Competitive as Business." *California Management Review* 44 (2002): 120–132.

Drayton, William. "Everyone a Changemaker." *Peer Review* 7 (2005): 8–12.

Drayton, William. "Letter to the Editor." *Stanford Social Innovation Review* 4 (2006): 5.

Elkington, John, and Pamela Hartigan. *The Power of Unreasonable People: How Social Entrepreneurs Create Markets That Change the World.* Boston: Harvard Business School Press, 2008.

Fleming, Lee. "Breakthroughs and the 'Long Tail' of Innovation." *MIT Sloan Management Review* 49 (2007): 69–74.

Francis, David, John Bessant, and Mike Hobday. "Managing Radical Organisational Transformation." *Management Decision* 41 (2003): 18–31.

Freeman, John, and Jerome S. Engel. "Models of Innovation: Startups and Mature Corporations." *California Management Review* 50 (2007): 94–119.

Gans, Joshua S., David H. Hsu, and Scott Stern. "When Does Start-Up Innovation Spur the Gale of Creative Destruction?" *RAND Journal of Economics* 33 (2002): 571–586.

Gartner, William B. "Some Suggestions for Research on Entrepreneurial Traits and Characteristics." *Entrepreneurship Theory and Practice* 13 (1989): 27–37.

Gartner, William B. "'Who Is an Entrepreneur?' Is the Wrong Question." *American Journal of Small Business* 12 (1988): 11–32.

Gartner, William B., Kelly G. Shaver, Elizabeth Gatewood, and Jerome A. Katz. "Finding the Entrepreneur in Entrepreneurship." *Entrepreneurship Theory and Practice* 18 (1994): 5–10.

Gupta, Vipin, Ian C. MacMillan, and Gita Surie. "Entrepreneurial Leadership: Developing and Measuring a Cross-Cultural Construct." *Journal of Business Venturing* 19 (2004): 241–260.

Harding, Rebecca. "Social Enterprise: The New Economic Engine." *Business Strategy Review* 15 (2004): 44–47.

Hargadon, Andrew B., and Douglas Yellowlees. "When Innovations Meet Institutions." *Administrative Science Quarterly* 46 (2001): 476–501.

Hayward, Mathew L. A., Dean A. Shepherd, and Dale Griffin. "A Hubris Theory of Entrepreneurship." *Management Science* 52 (2006): 160–172.

Heclo, Hugh. "Issue Networks and the Executive Establishment." In *The New American Political System,* edited by Anthony King, 87–124. Washington, DC: American Enterprise Institute, 1978.

Hellman, Thomas. "When Do Employees Become Entrepreneurs?" *Management Science* 53 (2007): 919–933.

Jelinek, Mariann, and Joseph A. Litterer. "Toward Entrepreneurial Organizations: Meeting Ambiguity with Engagement." *Entrepreneurship Theory and Practice* 20 (1995): 137–168.

Kaufmann, Daniel, and Aart Kraay. "Governance Indicators: Where Are We, Where Should We Be Going?" World Bank Policy Research Working Paper Series No. 4370, 2007.

Kerlin, Janelle A. "Social Enterprise in the United States and Europe: Understanding and Learning from the Differences." *Voluntas* 17 (2006): 247–263.

Kingdon, John. *Agendas, Alternatives, and Public Policies*. New York: Longman, 2002.

Kirkwood, Jodyanne. "Tall Poppy Syndrome: Implications for Entrepreneurship in New Zealand." *Journal of Management and Organization* 13 (2007): 366–382.

Kirzner, Israel M. "Creativity and/or Alertness: A Reconsideration of the Schumpeterian Entrepreneur." *Review of Austrian Economics* 11 (1999): 15–17.

Krueger, Norris F., Jr. "What Lies Beneath? The Experiential Essence of Entrepreneurial Thinking." *Entrepreneurship Theory and Practice* 31 (2007): 123–138.

LaFrance, Steven F. *Scaling Capacities: Supports for Growing Impact*. LaFrance Associates, July 2006.

Levin, Martin A., and Mary Bryna Sanger. *Making Government Work: How Entrepreneurial Executives Turn Bright Ideas into Real Results*. San Francisco: Jossey-Bass, 1994.

Light, Paul C. *The Four Pillars of High Performance: How Robust Organizations Achieve Extraordinary Results*. New York: McGraw-Hill, 2005.

Light, Paul C. *A Government Ill Executed: The Decline of the Federal Service and How to Reverse It*. Cambridge, MA: Harvard University Press, 2008.

Light, Paul C. *Government's Greatest Achievements: From Civil Rights to Homeland Defense*. Washington, DC: Brookings Institution Press, 2002.

Light, Paul C. *Pathways to Nonprofit Excellence*. Washington, DC: Brookings Institution Press, 2003.

Light, Paul C. "Reshaping Social Entrepreneurship." *Stanford Social Innovation Review* 4 (2006): 47–51.

Light, Paul C. *The Search for Social Entrepreneurship*. Washington, DC: Brookings Institution Press, 2008.

Light, Paul C. *Sustaining Innovation: Creating Nonprofit and Government Organizations That Innovate Naturally*. San Francisco: Jossey-Bass, 1998.

Light, Paul C. *Sustaining Nonprofit Performance: The Case for Capacity Building and the Evidence to Support It*. Washington, DC: Brookings Institution Press, 2004.

Light, Paul C. *The Tides of Reform: Making Government Work, 1945–1995*. New Haven, CT: Yale University Press, 1997.

Mair, Johanna, and Ignasi Marti. "Social Entrepreneurship: What Are We Talking About? A Framework for Future Research." Working paper, IESE Business School, University of Navarra, 2004.

Mair, Johanna, and Ignasi Marti. "Social Entrepreneurship Research: A Source of Explanation, Prediction, and Delight." *Journal of World Business* 41 (2006): 36–44.

Mair, Johanna, Jeffrey Robinson, and Kai Hockerts, eds. *Social Entrepreneurship*. New York: Palgrave, 2006.

Martin, Roger L. "To the Rescue: Beating the Heroic Leadership Trap." *Stanford Social Innovation Review* 1 (2003): 36–39.

Martin, Roger L., and Sally Osberg. "Social Entrepreneurship: The Case for Definition." *Stanford Social Innovation Review* 5 (2007): 29–39.

Moon, Myung Jae. "The Pursuit of Managerial Entrepreneurship: Does Organization Matter?" *Public Administration Review* 59 (1999): 31–43.

Morris, Michael H., Susan Coombes, Minet Schindehutte, and Jeffrey Allen. "Antecedents and Outcomes of Entrepreneurial and Market Orientations in a Non-Profit Context: Theoretical and Empirical Insights." *Journal of Leadership and Organizational Studies* 13 (2007): 12–36.

Mort, Gillian Sullivan, Jay Weerawardena, and Kashonia Carnegie. "Social Entrepreneurship: Towards Conceptualization." *International Journal of Nonprofit and Voluntary Sector Marketing* 8 (2003): 76–88.

Moynihan, Daniel P. "The Iron Law of Emulation." In *Counting Our Blessings: Reflections on the Future of America*, 115–137. Boston: Little, Brown, 1980.

Nicholls, Alex, ed. *Social Entrepreneurship: New Models of Sustainable Social Change*. Oxford: Oxford University Press, 2006.

O'Reilly, Charles A., III, and Michael L. Tushman. "The Ambidextrous Organization." *Harvard Business Review* 68 (2004): 74–81.

Peredo, Ana Maria, and Murdith McLean. "Social Entrepreneurship: A Critical Review of the Concept." *Journal of World Business* 41 (2006): 56–65.

Polley, Douglas, and Andrew H. Van de Ven. "Learning by Discovery during Innovation Development." *International Journal of Technology Management* 11 (1996): 871–883.

Putnam, Robert D. *Bowling Alone.* New York: Simon & Schuster, 2000.

Putnam, Robert D. "E Pluribus Unum: Diversity and Community in the Twenty-first Century. The 2006 Johan Skytte Prize Lecture." *Scandinavian Political Studies* 30 (2007): 137–174.

Rauch, Andrea, and Michael Frese. "Let's Put the Person Back into Entrepreneurship Research: A Meta-Analysis on the Relationship between Business Owner's Personality Traits, Business Creation, and Success." *European Journal of Work and Organizational Psychology* 16 (2007): 353–385.

Reich, Robert B. "Entrepreneurship Reconsidered: The Team as Hero." *Harvard Business Review* 65 (2001): 77–83.

Ronfeldt, David, John Arquilla, Graham Fuller, and Melissa Fuller. *The Zapatista "Social Netwar" in Mexico.* Los Angeles: RAND Corporation, 1998.

Schumpeter, Joseph A. *Business Cycles: A Theoretical, Historical, and Statistical Analysis of the Capitalist Process.* New York: McGraw-Hill, 1939.

Schumpeter, Joseph A. *Capitalism, Socialism, and Democracy.* New York: Harper & Brothers, 1942.

Schumpeter, Joseph A. *The Theory of Development.* Cambridge, MA: Harvard University Press, 1934.

Sen, Pritha. "Ashoka's Big Idea: Transforming the World through Social Entrepreneurship." *Futures* 39 (2007): 534–553.

Shane, Scott. *The Illusions of Entrepreneurship: The Costly Myths That Entrepreneurs, Investors, and Policy Makers Live By.* New Haven, CT: Yale University Press, 2008.

Shane, Scott, Edwin A. Locke, and Christopher J. Collins. "Entrepreneurial Motivation." *Human Resource Management Review* 13 (2003): 257–279.

Shane, Scott, and S. Venkataraman. "The Promise of Entrepreneurship as a Field of Research." *Academy of Management Review* 25 (2000): 217–226.

Sharp, Gene. *There Are Realistic Alternatives.* Boston: Albert Einstein Institution, 2003.

Shaw, Eleanor, and Sara Carter. "Social Entrepreneurship: Theoretical Antecedents and Empirical Analysis of Entrepreneurial Processes and Outcomes." *Journal of Small Business and Enterprise Development* 14 (2007): 418–434.

Simms, Shalei V. K., and Jeffrey Robinson. "Activist or Entrepreneur? An Identity-Based Model of Social Entrepreneurship." Submitted to USASBE 2006 Conference, August 15, 2005.

Simsek, Zeki, Michael H. Lubatkin, and Steven W. Floyd. "Inter-Firm Networks and Entrepreneurial Behavior: A Structural Embeddedness Perspective." *Journal of Management* 29 (2003): 427–442.

Singh, Jasjit and Lee Fleming. "Lone Inventors as Sources of Breakthrough: Myth or Reality?" *Management Science* 56 (2010): 41–56.

Singh, Smita, Patricia Corner, and Kathryn Pavlovich. "Coping with Entrepreneurial Failure." *Journal of Management and Organization* 13 (2007): 331–344.

Song, Michael, Ksenia Podoynitsyna, Hans van der Bij, and Johannes I. M. Halman. "Success Factors in New Ventures: A Meta-Analysis." *Journal of Product Innovation Management* 25 (2008): 7–27.

Spear, Roger. "Social Entrepreneurship: A Different Model." *International Journal of Social Economics* 33 (2006): 399–410.

Steiner, Carol J. "A Philosophy for Innovation: The Role of Unconventional Individuals in Innovation Success." *Journal of Product Innovation Management* 12 (1995): 431–440.

Thompson, John L. "The World of the Social Entrepreneur." *International Journal of Public Sector Management* 15 (2002): 412–431.

Thoreau, Henry David. *The Succession of Forest Trees and Wild Apples* (1887). Whitefish, MT: Kessinger Publishing, 2009.

Tushman, Michael L., and Charles A. O'Reilly III. "Ambidextrous Organizations: Managing Evolutionary and Revolutionary Change." *California Management Review* 38 (1996): 8–29.

Van de Venn, Andrew H. "The Development of an Infrastructure for Entrepreneurship." *Journal of Business Venturing* 8 (1993): 211–230.

Waddock, Sandra A., and James E. Post. "Social Entrepreneurs and Catalytic Change." *Public Administration Review* 51 (1991): 393–401.

Ward, Thomas B. "Cognition, Creativity, and Entrepreneurship." *Journal of Business Venturing* 19 (2003): 173–188.

Weerawardena, Jay, and Gillian Sullivan Mort. "Investigating Social Entrepreneurship: A Multidimensional Model." *Journal of World Business* 41 (2006): 21–35.

Weick, Karl. *Sensemaking in Organizations*. London: Russell Sage, 1995.

Weinberg, James, and Frances Kunreuther. *Conversations with Social Entrepreneurs: 2010 and Beyond*. Commongood Careers and Building Movement Project (2010), 2. Available at www.cgcareers.org/assets/pdf/Conversations_with_social_entrepreneurs.pdf.

Wei-Skillern, Jane, James E. Austin, Herman Leonard, and Howard Stevenson. *Entrepreneurship in the Social Sector.* Los Angeles: Russell Sage, 2007.

Wei-Skillern, Jane, and Sonia Marciano. "The Networked Nonprofit." *Stanford Social Innovation Review* 6 (2008): 39–43.

Wickham, Phillip A. "The Representativeness Heuristic in Judgments Involving Entrepreneurial Success and Failure." *Management Decision* 41 (2003): 156–167.

Wolf, Charles. *Looking Backward and Forward: Policy Issues in the Twenty-First Century.* Stanford, CA: Hoover, 2008.

Zhao, Hao, and Scott E. Seibert. "The Big Five Personality Dimensions and Entrepreneurial Status: A Meta-Analytic Review." *Journal of Applied Psychology* 91 (2006): 259–271.

Index